P9-CCB-122

Praise for *A New Garden Ethic*

A New Garden Ethic is an outstanding and deeply passionate book. Benjamin Vogt makes it clear that we need to expand our notion of "garden" to include all interconnected communities of all voiceless flora and fauna. We must rewild ourselves, reconnect with all of nature, and expand our compassion footprint. As Mr. Vogt aptly puts it, "It is time for daily wildness to be our calling. It is time for defiant compassion." This book is a game changer in an epoch I like to call "the rage of inhumanity." Alienation from nature is bad for everyone involved. We all need to coexist under a broad and inclusive umbrella of compassion.

—Marc Bekoff, author of *Rewilding Our Hearts* and *The Animals' Agenda: Freedom, Compassion, and Coexistence in the Age of Humans*

Benjamin Vogt writes with great passion about how our increasingly urbanized societies have lost the connection with the original landscapes in which we live. Not only do our cities have a "nature deficit", but in many cases the species of plants and animals we have introduced have been imported from geographies that do not represent the original indigenous ecosystems. This should concern us deeply. Our health and well-being depend on a strong connection with the natural world, and in particular on diverse communities of plants that have adapted to local climate and soils. The call to be conscious about what we plant in our gardens, and to respect the beauty and resilience of species that have been in our communities for millennia, is clear and urgent.

—Dr. Peter Robinson, Chief Executive Officer, David Suzuki Foundation

Our managed landscapes have forced nature out. If we garden with native plants, we can reconnect with nature providing sustenance for our souls and for wildlife. Benjamin Vogt's thought-provoking book, *A New Garden Ethic*, examines the historical, psychological, biological, and social reasons for why we urgently need balanced and equitable gardens that respect, support, and sustain all living things.

—Heather Holm, award-winning author of *Bees and Pollinators of Native Plants*

Benjamin Vogt gives us more than food for thought with *A New Garden Ethic*; he offers an entire wild ecosystem for mindful action. *A New Garden Ethic* makes as persuasive a case as can be made for gardens as radical—to the roots—ways of knowing the world and reckoning with our place in it. Vogt presents gardens as troubling sanctuaries of meaning, sites of ideological conflict, political statements, expressions of faith, places of cosmic connection, and dirt-under-the-nails realities of how we co-shape our world with other species. With beautiful description and insight, he explores how gardens can create social responsibility to a more-than-human world that is constantly speaking. Even as a person who has considered and questioned my own gardening goals, prior to reading this book I never imagined gardening could be so radical. Now I know. I'll never again look at any garden, or the planet, in the same way.

—Gavin Van Horn, Center for Humans and Nature
and coeditor of *Wildness: Relations of People and Place*

Benjamin Vogt makes a great case for gardening with compassion for the earth—its treasures and inhabitants. The treasure, here, are his words, and in rich prose, he reminds us that we won't find wealth and health for the future through destruction and consumption. He advises us to see our potential to be landscape stewards, to welcome wildlife, support and restore natural systems and in that way, enrich our lives as well.

—Ken Druse is a garden communicator and
the award-winning author/photographer of 20 books.

Native plant gardens matter! People, pollinators, birds, soil health, air and water quality, and our future are influenced by gardens. Vogt takes readers on a thoughtful and personal journey as he explores the power of gardens.

—Jennifer Hopwood, Senior Pollinator Conservation Specialist
at The Xerces Society for Invertebrate Conservation

In *A New Garden Ethic*, Benjamin Vogt lays out a compassionate and compelling case for welcoming nature in all of its messy diversity home to our yards, gardens, and domestic landscapes. This book is about so much more than gardening: Vogt shows how we can begin to heal our own wounds and those of our planet by opening ourselves to the value and beauty of the everyday wild, and the native plants that root us in place. A powerful and transformative work, written with honesty and grace.

—Susan J. Tweit, plant biologist, restoration gardener,
and award-winning author of *Walking Nature Home*

a new
garden ethic

a new
garden ethic

Cultivating Defiant Compassion
for an Uncertain Future

Benjamin Vogt

Copyright © 2017 by Benjamin Vogt.
All rights reserved.

Cover design by Diane McIntosh. Cover art © Benjamin Vogt.
p. 1 © Mark Herreid; p. 27 © leungchopan; p 63: © msurkamp;
p 137 © rabbit75_fot / Adobe Stock

Printed in Canada. Third printing May 2021.

Inquiries regarding requests to reprint all or part of *A New Garden Ethic* should be addressed to New Society Publishers at the address below. To order directly from the publishers, please call toll-free (North America) 1-800-567-6772, or order online at www.newsociety.com

Any other inquiries can be directed by mail to:

New Society Publishers
P.O. Box 189, Gabriola Island, BC V0R 1X0, Canada
(250) 247-9737

Library and Archives Canada Cataloguing in Publication

Vogt, Benjamin, 1976–, author
A new garden ethic : cultivating defiant compassion for
an uncertain future / Benjamin Vogt.

Includes bibliographical references and index.
Issued in print and electronic formats.
ISBN 978-0-86571-855-5 (softcover).—ISBN 978-1-55092-650-7
(PDF).—ISBN 978-1-77142-245-1 (EPUB)

1. Environmental ethics. 2. Endemic plants. 3. Gardening.
4. Human ecology. I. Title.

GE42.V64 2017   179.1   C2017-903767-6
                                                          C2017-903768-4

Funded by the   Financé par le
Government   gouvernement
of Canada   du Canada

Canada

New Society Publishers' mission is to publish books that contribute in fundamental ways to building an ecologically sustainable and just society, and to do so with the least possible impact on the environment, in a manner that models this vision.

new society
PUBLISHERS

Certified
B
Corporation

MIX
Paper from
responsible sources
FSC
www.fsc.org   FSC® C016245

Contents

It is the writer's duty to hate injustice,
to defy the powerful,
and to speak for the voiceless.

« EDWARD ABBEY »

Any genuine attempt by groups within society
to introduce change is viewed as a nuisance
based on romantic illusions
or an obstacle to be circumvented.

« POPE FRANCIS »

—

A work of art opens a void,
a moment of silence,
a question without answer,
provokes a breach without reconciliation
where the world is forced to question itself.

« MICHEL FOUCAULT »

CHAPTER 1

A New
Garden Ethic

Acknowledging our love for the living
world does something that a library full of
papers on sustainable development and
ecosystem services cannot: it engages
the imagination as well as the intellect.

—GEORGE MONBIOT

A COMMON YELLOW garden spider has draped her web beside a birch tree and above New England asters and Virginia mountain mint. It's autumn and the asters are still in bloom, their almost gaudy pink petals guiding insects to the yellow pollen at their center, while the mountain mint is two months past bloom, its gray, pockmarked seed heads like small asteroids perched precariously atop telephone poles. In the mornings, dewdrops balance on every blade and filament of leaf and bloom, every silken thread of web, and every branch tip. By lunchtime the landscape spins with insects on wobbly ziplines, invisible paths etched by more than faith or hope, and far greater than simple purpose; it's as if the world is stenciling itself a design to follow.

On afternoons I make my rounds, noticing how each day brings invigorating new changes to the garden, subtle in the memory but sharp in the moment. The Sun is low in the south, but it's still incredibly warm as it penetrates into the darker areas beneath birch and oak; out in the open, early fallen elm leaves are dry and disintegrate like potato chips underfoot, but in the shade they are damp and slick, holding tight to the places they cover.

While bees, flies, and moths work the late-season blooms, holdover grasshoppers spring like traps—each one excited by my snaking among the tight paths of this made-up world. Between the open sun of the main garden and the long depths of the side garden, I stop to visit the spider. Her web is empty and shows no signs of prey, not even a torn area she's been unable to repair. This goes on for days. An empty web perfectly formed, speckled with light and dusted by evening with blazingstar seed.

Without thinking too much about it—and with as much curiosity as I've ever had—I stalk a grasshopper in some nearby foliage. I work from behind where its eyesight is probably poorest, present an open hand two feet away, close in, and quickly cup it in my palm. It's not easy to overcome my reaction to hurl it through the air; its thumping, jumping, and scraping against my skin tickles uncomfortably like sandpaper. Running over to the web, I take aim and toss the undulating grasshopper. It frees itself one leg at a time, but then gets stuck again as it drops. That's when the spider darts, injects the grasshopper with venom, spins it in silk, and holds the body still against itself. Over the course of a few weeks, I repeat this ritual many times, failing as often as I succeed, engrossed in the way life becomes life.

But then I begin to feel troubled. Slowly, it seems clear I'm committing nothing short of murder. I might as well be poisoning my backyard with a fogger or tossing grenades into the plants. What have I done, forcing my will upon another living creature? Did I really ever believe that I was helping the spider through some act of compassion? Why did I connect more emotionally with the spider than the grasshopper? I had no right to choose which creature was more valuable, judging which had more worth to live by interfering in a natural process. I gave into my craving to see nature be nature for my own immediate gratification, too impatient or unwilling to sit by that web for hours waiting—and in the process probably learning far more than I could imagine. This garden isn't nature. Even though I find necessary solace, comfort, and even pain here, I am no more a part of the wild echo than I was before the garden came along.

It's autumn I always crave, suffering through the torment of a slow spring, and then the sugary exuberance of bloom after bloom in the unending summer heat laden with mosquitoes and leaf blowers. Autumn is cold mornings frosting the leaves, warm afternoons fueling the wildlife, cool evenings sprinkled with distant smoke that sticks to my sweater for days. Autumn is the call of snow geese migrating far above; fresh swallowtails rising from dark places to lay one more brood of eggs; and then, eventually, a growing absence. I think it's the absence I love most about nature—the way clouds and foxes and bees are given definition simply by passing through a wide-open moment. It's the idea of negative space, I suppose, that the empty space or absence around an object lends profound meaning to that object. In drawing and painting, an artist makes the shadows first to create trees or stones, and perhaps this is what life is—shadows and voids creating what we interpret as feeling and nature, the real stuff we hold on to. It's not the ironweed or the bee that gives meaning, it's their having been in a moment then suddenly gone in the next. In autumn, and then in winter, the absence is so profound you can hear snowflakes hitting the ground, little paper jewels like a slow tide coming in.

While it's our presence in the form of gardens that brings nature to our urban lives, it's the wake or echo of our beliefs that lingers and reverberates the longest. The choices we make and the rules or feelings we live by create our gardens as much as the plants that inhabit them. In essence, our values are the negative space that gives landscapes their cultural definition, and in turn, guide our social and environmental principles. What we honor now in our landscapes is what will give life to future generations of humans, plants, and animals.

We know we have an innate "passionate love of life and of all that is alive," as psychoanalyst Erich Fromm put it in 1973. Fromm labeled this phenomenon "biophilia," a term popularized by E. O. Wilson a decade later. Wilson insinuated there's a genetic basis for our subconscious desire to affiliate with nature. This desire is really only a weak biological urge, but it can be exercised to become more than muscle memory as we learn about nature—and especially as we spend time in it, whether we're walking a restored prairie, a wild wetland, or garden beds along city streets. Our biophilia can lead to deep emotional connection, a lifelong job, or passionate activism. For all but the most recent century, our species has lived in wilder environments, but 70 to 80 percent of us will soon live in or near cities. What does urban life do, not only to our psyche but to our biology, when we are more cut off from nature, from daily interactions with wildness? And maybe more importantly, what happens to our ethical codes and our ability to perceive larger changes in the environment, from longer growing seasons to fewer songbirds and butterflies? What happens to our response to the suffering and love of others—not just of other species, but even among our own?

There are two core philosophies that describe how we interact with and engage nature and environment.[1] The first is deep ecology, which explores the very heart of our environmental issues by directly challenging personal and societal values—which can be highly uncomfortable and even psychologically painful. Deep ecology wants to revamp the human systems that deny cultural diversity and biodiversity in nature, recognizing human culture as not the only or even primary culture. The second philosophy is shallow ecology, which promotes technological fixes to environmental issues, often using the same methods as a consumptive, industrial-based society that eroded nature. The main difference between both philosophies is that deep ecology regards all species as having essential wisdom to guide us forward, whereas shallow ecology primarily looks to humans for understanding and direction.

In a human-dominated world, we can't deny one philosophy for the other—they can and should work together. And both philosophies also share a common trait in biophilia, even if their approaches are different. The challenge before us is to not just embrace shallow ecology as we exercise our biophilia. The technology already exists to make a profound difference on our impact on biodiversity, even if our political and cultural systems impede the technological applications. The true challenge, and the greatest opportunity, is in seeing all life as equal, all life as contributing to our culture and our homes, and all life as essential to the health and future of our nations. The challenge will be a change in our empathy and compassion, a rewiring of our society that supercharges our latent love for nature.

What this challenge boils down to is a new ethic—a landscape ethic—and in our cities, a garden ethic. This garden ethic is derived from Aldo Leopold's land ethic, as he relates in his book *A Sand County Almanac*:

> The land ethic simply enlarges the boundaries of the community to include soils, waters, plants, and animals, or collectively: the land.... That land is a community is the basic concept of ecology, but that land is to be loved and respected is an extension of ethics.... A land ethic, then, reflects the existence of an ecological conscience, and this in turn reflects a conviction of individual responsibility for the health of land.... We can be ethical only in relation to something we can see, feel, understand, love, or otherwise have faith in.... A land ethic changes the role of *Homo sapiens* from conqueror of the land-community to plain member and citizen of it...it implies respect for his fellow-members, and also respect for the community as such.

Leopold's ideas on environmental fraternity have radically influenced how we see, work with, and manage large tracts of wilderness and near wilderness. And while he is radical in that he presents a philosophy that's in opposition to our mainstream society of ownership and possession, Leopold is radical in another sense as well—in getting down to the root of our understanding, our care, and our innate love or connection with wildness. In a society that sees wildness as sometimes threatening, or as something to be used in a brief moment for our pleasure or profit, Leopold insists we experience daily wildness as the more-than-real shadow that gives our lives definition and meaning—wildness is at the core of our joy and sorrow, it balances us as it tips us over.

Where we get into trouble with a landscape ethic or garden ethic, though, is the very word itself: *ethic*. Years ago I used the word *moral*, but it is many times more problematic than *ethic*, for it implies a rash judgment of puritanical undertones, a distinct if not damning "right" or "wrong." By using the term *ethics*, we open ourselves up to a larger dialogue that is not so much critical as it is practicing critical thinking, or deep ecology. This deeper thinking is what the Aldo Leopold Foundation explores in how we define and use the term *ethics*, specifically in two ways. The first is the idea that ethics help us decide how to live. The Foundation proclaims "they [our ethics] are prescriptive in that they tell us what we should or ought to do and which values we should or ought not hold. They also help us evaluate whether something is good or bad, right or wrong."

Ethics are also useful in explaining why wildlife and landscapes are important or valuable, and in describing the actions we can take to demonstrate those values. In other words, our ethical perspective is not just informed by one ideology such as economics or beauty, but by multiple perspectives at once that take into account the larger shared community; think on how a marsh not only filters drinking water and reduces flooding but is also home to wrens and frogs and snakes and lightning bugs. That marsh might also be a place of historical value, or reflect some sense of regional identity or pride. What personal values are being followed in the actions we take toward the marsh, and are those actions in line with our beliefs?

Somewhere in the mess of these two definitions is a garden ethic; one that links the human and nonhuman, the urban and the wild, the present and the future, and binds us to one another as part of a mutually supportive community. But if we can stretch ourselves further—if we can strive and even succeed in seeing our world through the eyes of another species—we'll be able to go further than if we just agree that other lives are important, or everyone deserves a fair shake. What happens when other species are primary and humans are secondary, if even for a moment? What happens when landscapes stop being mostly for us, but are split more fairly between all species that give meaning to our country, our state, our city, and our homes? What happens when we put the good of others before our own immediate good? In love, as in a successful business, providing what someone else needs provides us with what we need, even if it takes a long time to see that benefit. If we decide not to convert a grassland to corn, not to put in a concrete median in favor of ornamental plantings, not to have a 100 percent lawn landscape around our house, we are making conscious decisions that benefit more than the immediate bottom line or a default mode of aesthetics. Over time, we are providing for the very real environmental needs not only of ourselves, but of other species as well.

Some argue that it's not realistic to expect humans to see through another creature's perspective, or to expect large, meaningful changes that revolutionize how gardens function. And yet, if we reach for an impossible dream, the improbable becomes more likely. Our reach must always exceed our grasp if we wish to achieve worthwhile objectives. We have to displace our sense of entitlement in all that we do, and have to start getting comfortable gardening with a viewpoint that is not entirely human. To be truly liberated, we have to be beholden to the functioning world, and to each other through its thriving biodiversity. For example, we should strive to make landscapes that are not only attractive and useful to us, but that are equally if not more attractive and useful to other species. Such a goal cannot be achieved by taking careful steps over decades, not if we are sensitive to the immediate realities of changing weather patterns, vanishing wildlife, and pollution; these larger environmental issues need radical thinking, dreaming, and action on an order of magnitude that inspires us deeply and profoundly instead of teasing out our latent biophilia in small increments. We need urban gardens that exuberantly embrace wildness in its complex fullness, not in a watered-down echo that does us little good.

I don't want to live in a hollowed-out world, physically, emotionally, or psychologically. I don't want to know what it's like not hearing the arching cadence of a bobwhite in the nearby woods, or not being lost in the thick tallgrass where a majority of monarchs reproduce on milkweed each summer. Time and again I hear how native plant landscapes aren't possible, that it's necessary to meet people where they are, gently encouraging the addition of a few native plants here and there over time, or slowly removing lawn from public spaces. The implication is that one can go too far, too fast. This means we can't quickly expect anyone to embrace an urban garden that's lushly layered and brimming with wildlife, or one composed of plants from the local ecoregion that wildlife must have, or one that eschews thin foundation beds around homes filled with rock mulch that dries out soil. Where people are, though, is stuck in a culture that extracts life from the planet to satiate fleeting pleasure. Where people are is in a planet that can't wait another minute for us to wake up to our potential to be more than we allow ourselves within the warped systems we've created.

Without presenting viable options, without aiming for more than we hoped, how will anyone know another way? If our landscapes all look the same from state to state and country to country—using the same plants in the same ways—we lose our sense of self, place, and compassion for the community as a whole. In this spirit, we'll need plants that coevolved with fauna to revive life, and native plant gardens that emulate their wild origins to create a function that goes beyond supporting butterflies, cleaning water, or cooling the air. Native plant gardens bring the places we escape to on weekends or annual vacations into every moment; they make us part of the global language again by rooting us into a community. Native plant gardens awaken and exercise biophilia on levels we're just beginning to quantify but have always felt. That reviving wildness with native plant landscapes isn't realistic may be a perception of a society stuck in a system of manipulation instead of cooperation, and a lack of social ethics that more of us are crying out for today.

It's in the muck and mire where we often grow the most. In doubt and confusion, the untouchable and even the putrid—in those moments and feelings that at first feel alien but can become so life-giving. As a child I didn't play in the dirt or raise caterpillars or bring decomposing animals into the house. More than one photo shows me squatting like a baseball catcher above mud or grass, carefully pinching a stone or a twig between my small fingers. I was afraid of every creepy crawly, from worms and spiders to birds and fish. Even when I was much older, I was careful not to slide across the ground, constantly aware of getting dirty. When I began gardening on my own as a thirty-something adult, those walls broke down. Slowly, I relished the cracking dirt molded to my back and arms that had mixed with liters of sweat. I wore the same ratty jeans day after day. I even wore shorts to expose my hairy legs and began taking my shirt off then washing myself down with hose water. If you'd known me before, you'd not have recognized the seemingly crazed guy gutting out a 95-degree afternoon. I was nasty with the earth.

Maybe I've just grown up or grown more comfortable in my skin, or maybe having a garden—literally bleeding in a place—has stirred something I never knew I possessed. I've raised monarch, swallowtail, and sulphur butterfly caterpillars for years now. I've touched their excrement and their diseased bodies, and I've held their liquefied remains eaten by tachinid fly larvae. I've carried spiders from kitchen to garden with guarded ease. I've buried birds covered in maggots. And I've pulled myself back from the soil with the speed of light when a centipede started working its way up my arm. Sometimes, I'll go outside to divide a plant just before I know a rainstorm will arrive, soaking up the still afternoon as darkness grows and thunder spills closer. It's this unknown, this almost dangerous and certainly unfamiliar wildness, which gives me comfort in my pain and pain in my comfort. I go to the garden to be consumed, redistributed, and rebuilt without having to lose my life; every part of the natural world, from the "ugly" to the "pretty," makes me more human.

Gardens are one primary way to connect to the world, to lift the veil of our emotions, fears, and desires while holding a dialogue with the environment and species whose language we have lost over time. Each garden places us firmly within the context of all life, awakens us to the web, humbles us as we become aware of ourselves as a node in that interlinked web. When we touch the soil, we touch our ancestors and our children, we know the heartbeats of worms, birds, insects, and mammals with each scrape of the nail and each cut of the skin. The taste of our own flesh is in soil. When we nestle a plant into a newly dug hole, we are reaching out to bees that will gather pollen and frogs that will take shelter in a rainstorm. A garden is our grasping for the world as much as it is a giving to the world—who are we, where have we been, where we will go. A garden is the moment, now, every emotion, every bit of knowing and unknowing coalescing into a timeless equality of mind, body, and spirit. In our best moments, we are no less than a garden that serves life, not ourselves.

So many of our landscapes are a no-man's-land, scarred and abused, forgotten and misunderstood—remnants of our lack of knowledge or connection. They are absent of substance. Too many of our landscapes are made up of a single culture, a single species, a single way of looking at the natural world, all at the expense of biodiversity. Our suburban and urban planting areas are especially devoid of life, ecological function, and a sense of ethical interaction with the world; in some ways parks, arboretums, and botanical gardens also present a type of ethics that shows a deep divide between species and place, so much so that it's hard to imagine any meaningful sense of biophilia exists.

Our manicured and unused lawns are inflammatory words hurled at the planet, places where we forcibly cast out life.[2] Foundation beds along homes, businesses, schools, and churches are sculpture gardens for a few misplaced, mismatched specimens a landscaper had left over from another job or were on sale at the supplier. Parking lots rush oily water filled with trash to clog storm drains and foul streams and lakes, instead of settling toward bioswales or rain gardens to be cleaned and filtered by plants evolved to do the job for free.

We live in a world of perfectly spaced plants that mimic headstones aligned in exact intervals. Wood mulch is more important to us than flowers. We clean up our gardens like they are living rooms after the children have gone to bed. We mow the world back on roadsides, hellstrips, business frontages, vacant lots, and parklands, beating any sense of wonder, awe, or love into submission. We've even set up laws that mandate this sort of forced submission upon nature to the point that any deviation from this norm is believed to be highly seditious, unpatriotic, undemocratic, and worth getting reported by a neighbor. And yet, Leopold reminds us, "nonconformity is the highest evolutionary attainment of social animals." For a species to evolve and grow, it must constantly be challenged from within and without; not conforming to social norms will help us foster healthy and necessary biodiversity. Our world is asking for gardens to be more, to light the way to a new relationship with nature, to be radical in their roots and their blooms.

While we treat our landscapes as simplified places and grudgingly necessary ornamentation, we also treat our more ornate public gardens as pieces of static art to experience, briefly ponder, and enjoy, then leave behind for the next physical stimulus. We treat plants like pieces of jewelry, fine dresses, and designer shoes, with the newest trend most proudly displayed in magazines and social media pages. Instead of celebrating plants as parts of a global community, and highlighting what each can do for life beyond our own visual pleasure, we focus exclusively on a new leaf color or a new bloom shape, seldom considering or knowing how these alterations affect other species or the larger community or the repercussions of our choices over time. And while we may need the kind of aesthetic beauty gardens deliver in order to connect with nature, plants are far more than a visual commodity.

Simply put, plants are not art. What we do with them, how we honor their life processes as part of creating ecological function—that's art. It's frustrating when the talk is so often focused on how pretty a plant looks, not on what its deeper contribution is to life above and below the soil line. Our lives will vastly improve on many levels if we ogle a plant not just because we find it attractive but also because it's covered in larvae or supports beneficial soil bacteria. We've got to stop judging a plant by its cover and look beyond what it does for us alone. Plants are not for us. We just presume this to be the case because we live in a culture that views humans as primary, superior and all other life—all other intelligence—as secondary, here to be used only for our benefit.

Ultimately, the natural world is not here to look pretty for us. It does not exist in order to be decorated with statements of our exaltation of its beauty. That we find it so moving is a product of our biology, our linked genetics—call it a stewardship gene or at the very least a shared purpose. Nature is not something to extract resources from—whether that be in the form of fuel or as inspiration for paintings and gardens. The natural world doesn't need us, even though we may be part of the evolution of life figuring itself out. That we think nature needs us—that we assume we are fundamental to the functioning of life—is what alienates us from life and keeps us from becoming something far more. Because we can decode DNA or cure diseases or send people to the Moon is not evidence of our greatness, but evidence of nature's greatness in giving birth to us. Every organism on Earth is here not *for* us but *with* us, and the loss of a single species by our hands—whether through damming rivers, deforestation, or carbon dioxide in the atmosphere—is an eradication of our own being.

Beauty is a fluid concept that strives to give clear definition to what we feel—what we love and fear, what we desire and despise. A garden as a setting for humans is beautiful only insofar as it helps us mitigate the more violent aspects of our culture and brings us into a deeper understanding of shared relationships across species. Gardens are not pretty. Gardens are not useful. Gardens are an orphaned species trying hard to find its way back home through the maze of its own culture, unsure of how to make sense of the journey or even how to make it. Gardens are essential tools to help us reimagine this epoch of humanity: the Anthropocene.[3]

Since we've created a soup of altered climate and threatened species, the world is now a garden we must manage to preserve some of its biological integrity—an unfortunate state of reality we've forced ourselves into. If the entire planet is a garden, how are we going to care for it? Should we? What will be the guiding principles? Will the world be just for us and our sense of beauty? Or will we open our hearts and minds and rethink beauty—a deeper, functional beauty designed for species and environments other than our own? The more we check our egos at the garden gate, the more we'll make gardens that work for a common good, that reconnect us to the world we're erasing, and even bring us closer to one another.

Ultimately, if gardens are art, maybe it's in the spirit of art as an attempt to express the inexpressible, a way to bridge how we interpret the world emotionally, how we internalize and experience life, what we value in our most authentic moments of reflection and connection. Art as a revolution, perhaps. And yet many gardens and greenscapes—places most folks call nature—are not meaningful nature in the biophilic sense, and certainly not in the ecological, practical, or ethical sense. When gardens aren't supporting local flora and fauna—life endemic to that place and pushed to the margins—they fail to be the models of democracy and freedom we imagine them to be. A designed landscape that does not see beyond the human is a landscape devoid of the human. It's devoid of forgiveness, mercy, hope, equality, and community.

It's essential to rethink our gardens, to probe their meanings and expose how and why we make them, to question and hopefully invigorate the world we alter. When you walk through a garden, what is your first response? What is your second response? What do you leave with? Are you first overrun by your senses, by color and texture and shape and scent? Do you stay focused on the cacophony of color and texture, or are you also able to slow down and focus on a moment, a microcosm of life within the landscape? How long do you linger? Why do you go? Are you motivated after you leave, underwhelmed, overwhelmed?

A designer plans for texture and intrigue, as well as how water moves through a landscape and how people use the space. A garden proclaims status as well as belief. Lawn, walls, the number of trees, the arrangement of plants, all are an aesthetic of both emotion and culture. Since gardens are human-centered creations, too often ecology and wildlife get only lip service or greenwashing to appeal to social trends or the marketplace. By extension, the idea that plants and wildlife first and foremost must bring us pleasure limits our sense of wonder as well as the independent lives of other species, not to mention our sense of right and wrong. For example, is it right to place a plant in our garden beds however we see fit, without considering its natural associations with other plants, soil life, and fauna? Is it right to place that plant without considering its needs as primary, and the needs of the ecosystem it is entering or creating as more important than our own?

If a biophilic garden begins with the pretty or beautiful—a fairly subjective sense defined by both an individual and their culture—then it shows the human eye as arrogant. A garden is then a negotiation between our arrogance and the perceived arrogance of a wildness we constantly battle. Gardens tend to fight back wildness and make it legible; they mold nature into something we understand and are comfortable with. But in that victory of conquering nature through gardening, we lose a deeper understanding of wildness and ourselves. We set up ourselves and our gardens as an ideal, one that excludes deeper levels of meaning. As we cultivate this shallow ideal, we might feel that something is awry. It's the imperfection or incongruity of our actions we grow uncomfortable with—our inability to feel safe within or be part of the natural community, how our concrete and oil and pesticides work to subdue nature and ease our alienation from it. The art of a garden is the simultaneous practice of immersion and avoidance, of gardening for life and against it. Yet what is art but at first a very personal, and then ultimately very public, struggle with our place in the world and our understanding of what it means to be an apex species—one with a fluid ethical code dictated by emotion?

Maybe what it comes down to is this: if the primary and essential way we see the world is through aesthetic experience, then we've denied power and efficacy to our other senses, as well as to our relation to the larger web of life. Our gardens say a lot about our belief in ourselves and the natural world, about who and what we respect. Gardens have deep meaning when they are created and managed to benefit other species, even other humans. Shifting the perspective beyond our own can feel strange and disruptive. But art should be disruptive. And being composed of other sentient, living organisms with their own distinct life processes, gardens have value and meaning beyond their artistic representation. Why we make them and how we design them reveals the extent of our social responsibility, as well as our awareness of how the world works and what ecology really is.

Gardening from a larger-than-human perspective can also be empowering. In this time of climate disruption and mass extinction, gardens are becoming places of activism, where we work to get at the root of our disconnect with nature and each other while rocking the boat. This is obvious in urban food forests, community vegetable gardens, and even more so in front yards turned to meadows, sitting areas, or anything other than unused conventional lawn. Activism of any sort always makes another group uncomfortable—that's part of the point. Radical ideas can always appear to undermine the status quo, ideas and beliefs we accept or trust blindly because they've seemingly always existed and appear stable or trustworthy. An activist seeks to question the validity of a belief or a circumstance, to test that validity against an ethical code, and to either accept or rewrite the beliefs and codes based on new information and experience. Such an activist will run toward conflict and debate in an eagerness to refuse what's been given to them, to not accept at face value something they feel is unjust. And such a person will present a new perspective to others that doesn't necessarily invalidate a counterpoint, even though the first emotional response will be to think that's the case.

I'm reminded of what Kumi Naidoo, past executive director of Greenpeace, said about the origins of the organization being anti-Vietnam-War Quakers who believed in bearing witness: "If there's an injustice in the world, those of us that have the ability to witness it and to record it, document it and tell the world what is happening, have a moral responsibility to do that. Then, of course, it's left up to those that are receiving that knowledge to make the moral choice about whether they want to stand up against the injustice or observe it." In this vein we have an ethical responsibility to reflect on what is and isn't happening in our gardens, even if that makes those who adhere to the status quo uncomfortable.

We live with an echo that reverberates back and forth between landscape and human culture, between cropland and cheap food, between action and hope, between health and sickness. How we treat each other and ourselves is reflected in the landscape, in our gardens. As we erode diversity of species and places, we erode not only nature's resiliency but our own. The greatest injustice of our time may be the eradication of native ecosystems, the erasure of entire life forms, and the capacity of one species to ignore those injustices. Wildness is that which we fear to hold close to us, for it might show how far apart we are from one another.

Every time I plant a milkweed, I both interrupt and intercede in the world—I hinder and help in the same action. My act of making a sustainable urban garden is a remaking of nature, a way to connect myself through proof and belief that I have the power to heal us all, to move deeper into the cycles of life even as I disrupt or alter them in the garden and in every aspect of my modern Western life. I drive a car that uses gasoline to pick up new plants or a needed tool. I order supplies from a distant business that uses fossil fuels to package and ship those supplies. I heat my home with natural gas, the production of which poisons groundwater, shakes the Earth, and erodes wildlife habitat. Even my garden clothes are polyester blends, plastics made from oil that slowly break apart in the wash and accumulate in the bodies of aquatic species. And that's where modern life gets problematic. One myth of a garden is that it rights systemic cultural wrongs such as human supremacy or capitalism or deforestation—that we help the environment, get in tune with nature, and inherently practice sustainability simply by using plants. Another myth of the garden is that any garden, any composition of plants, is better than no garden at all—that it doesn't really matter if you use a large proportion of native plants or not as long as the plants you use are fitted to the soil, light, and climatic conditions. Sure, the thinking goes, native plants are an important component, but a successful garden's main benefit is to sustain itself with little input from us while maintaining its aesthetic value.

Too many of our human political and cultural beliefs are imprinted on our gardens and their nonhuman inhabitants. Plants and bees are not people, and their culture is radically different from ours; yet like every other minority—from prairie dogs to Native American tribes—we impose the dominant culture on them in myriad ways. We are colonizers who replace the culture of the oppressed with the culture of the oppressor, whether that's through our plant choices or in how we arrange those plants. A garden can be a way to bridge our seemingly disparate cultures, but it's also often a way to exercise domination over others in the name of one's own joy, happiness, and sense of personal freedom. If this control is primarily what a garden is, then perhaps gardens will, in the end, always fail to move us into a better relationship with other species and ecosystems.

Author Joy Williams notes that "the ecological crisis cannot be resolved by politics. It cannot be resolved by science or technology. It is a crisis caused by culture and character, and a deep change in personal consciousness is needed.... This is essentially a moral issue we face, and moral decisions must be made." Our gardens are not free of ethical consideration. They are a part of nature even if they don't often function naturally, and how we make them will always be a direct reflection of what we value. We have to choose what gardens mean and what they are to be, and perhaps in doing so, fundamentally change our worldview through the lens of garden making itself. But are we capable of doing so?

Ultimately, our cultural and personal assumptions make us feel safe. They provide a sense of order and predictability around a wild life we feel is chaotic and could turn on us at any moment. These feelings stem from our hard work to disconnect ourselves from nature and its processes, rhythms, ebbs, and flows—for example, through lives lived indoors and being unaware of how our food is produced. Our massive and complicated brains provide us the ability to transcend existence through reflection and thinking outside the box; this is how we can not only perform complex tasks but also analyze them abstractly. If we build a new shed out back, we're not just thinking about how to do it and what it will look like; we're also thinking about what it will feel like in the landscape, what it will be like looking out from inside, and how we might use the shed in different ways years down the road. We might even consider who else will use the shed after we are gone, or how it exemplifies who we are.

Of course, our brains can also lead us to alienate ourselves from the world—especially since they are programmed or evolutionarily hardwired to see chaos as a threat to our survival. The irony is that what we perceive as threatening chaos is really supreme cosmic

order. Everything, from dark forests to deep oceans and seasons
to even time itself, is magnificently ordered. And yet anything
we can't comprehend in an instant through simple, non-abstract
thought is labeled chaotic by our first, instinctual response. But we
are more than our instincts. We are also evolutionarily hardwired
by our experience of beauty and other emotion-driven judgments,
programmed to experience them in ways defined by what our culture shares in media and what we experience in our daily lives from
birth to death. Our first touch and other sensory encounters shape
how we touch and process the world from then on. Our first tactile experiences with a perfume or a wool blanket are how we will
forever experience perfume and wool blankets—and this is how
we process beauty as well as comfort, as well as every other emotionally defined experience. Beauty as an occurrence or an idea is
shaped by our religion, our parents, our friends, and our teachers,
as well as by how much money we have to access physical beauty,
or to have the leisure time to think philosophically about it.

Of course a garden must be pretty. Our cityscapes and suburban homes, our urban parks and roadsides, all of these must share
in our cultural idea of pretty if we are to maintain a sense of social
cohesion that comforts us. Our vision and other senses are what
draw us into a place, give us the feeling of repose or joy or safety
that we seek. We prefer landscapes that appeal to our animal
instincts; we desire to be protected by cover and to see danger
approaching from a distance. Maybe we tend to insist on open
lawns and meadows in more public or unfamiliar places because
we have a primal wariness about what might be lurking around the
corner. However, in our home landscapes, safe behind fences and
in places we walk every day, we may tend to yearn for seclusion,
shadows, and cloistered sitting areas, places where we can let our
guard down.

Our culture dictates that a pretty garden is an easily legible one.
For some people, this expectation of legibility also extends to wild
landscapes, but because of our disconnection from nature, wild
places are less and less legible to us. We do not readily perceive

order behind the seeming chaos unless and until we accumulate ecological knowledge, which helps us understand and recognize natural patterns and processes.

Finding reliable patterns helps us hold on to our reality and feel safe, and then even joyful. When visiting a garden, we first see and hold onto basic patterns of repeated form, color, and texture. Yet what makes us feel safe and joyful often diminishes the safety and joy of other species. There is an opportunity in balancing the seemingly disparate needs of our own instincts against the comfort (or presence) of other species. We can stretch our own definition of what is comfortable in a wilder garden, allowing a deeper connection with nature if we are willing to temper our instinctive responses. If we can ask our gardens to be more, then maybe we can be more—maybe we can refocus who we are and become greater than we dreamed.

We are in the midst of an evolutionary rewiring as we come out of our species' relative infancy on the planet. The industrial revolution—the industrialization of life—is calling into question our physical and psychological balance with nature. The juncture of personal desire and an ethics of expansive, inclusionary existence for all life is invigorating our response to the environment and our role in it. We are experiencing growing pains as we delve into ethical issues in landscape design, just as we are experiencing them in conversations around gender, religion, and race. We are becoming more than animal as we struggle to find out how animal we really are.

Gardens console us, welcome us, connect us. They bring us moments of peace and reflection. They help us doubt. They humble. They teach. They make us smarter. They heal. Because gardens do so much for us, they can be at the center of rethinking our ethics for nature and beyond. Unfortunately, we also idealize our gardens, place them on a pedestal so magnificent they almost seem untouchable and impervious to critique or change. We need more mindfulness in gardens. I wish every gardener could spend a week sitting by a sunflower observing every insect, every interaction, every raindrop and breeze that affects the plant. If we could see the garden through the perspective of a sunflower, would we become different gardeners? How would our practice change? How would our interactions with flora and fauna, with humans, morph in the coming months and years?

A garden is not at any stage a pristine Eden, and neither is nature. It is not a place of exclusion or seclusion. A garden is not an idealization of perfection or a perfected idealization. A garden is not for me, but is a nexus of everything I did not understand or realize before I had a garden—other lives, other needs, other moments.

A garden, once created, is a selfless expression of faith as processes beyond my control are set in motion. A garden is created not with self as the centering, ordering property, but as everything else as centering and ordering—as the passing shadows of other lives given definition and shape by the deeper reality of the landscape.

A garden will never quite be nature, and it will always be limited by our conception and perception of what nature is in our eye at one moment in time. A garden is an interpretation, and as a result is as fallible as we are in our knowledge and beliefs, which change through discovery and practice. But just as we can and should evolve, the garden can and should evolve. When I look out my window into the garden, I don't see myself as instigator or even creator. In the end I hope to not even see myself at all. The garden is the sunflower turning to face the daylight, pollen in the bloom and nectar along the stem that attracts ants and butterflies and bees and beetles. The sunflower is the instigator and creator. The sunflower is the moment a garden ceases to be a garden and becomes a conduit to freedom from the tyranny of our human-made reality, a reality too often divorced from nature.

It's another autumn in the main garden I started nine years ago. It's the second autumn for the front-yard prairie garden and the first autumn for the new backyard meadow that I sowed and planted directly into the lawn. Already the oldest garden is like my fifteen-year-old cat—dependable, loyal, communicative, punctual, and a true friend. The other gardens, well, I'm not too sure what they are—wild kittens who need a guiding hand and who are teaching me that such a hand doesn't have to be so direct, that in fact I'm the one being taught.

Out front along the avenue of concrete and short-clipped lawns, my little designed meadow of native grasses and flowers sways with butterflies, moths, bees, and wasps. I was careful to keep plants only one to two feet high within six feet of the side-walk, to use drifts and masses of taller grasses like little bluestem and flowers like rattlesnake master. Asters gone to seed give themselves into the air like puffs of inverse snow, all in the form of tiny wings pulsing against the wind. In late summer monarchs and skippers weave themselves around the spires of rough blazing-star seeking nectar, and goldfinches carve open the darkened seed heads of coneflower, calling out in sharp alarm as I walk to the mailbox. I startled a prairie toad one day who was resting in a clump of bristleleaf sedge. Invigorated by the wildlife using the new space, I tore out the dogwood shrub that was in too much shade and put in an entire sedge bed with autumn-blooming calico aster, careful to weave my way around a small hole that launched foraging yellow jackets into the sky.

Out back in the new two-thousand-foot meadow, I added another three hundred or so juvenile plants—nodding onion, smooth aster, pale purple coneflower, ironweed, and poppy mallow. Already last fall's hundred plugs are bringing in pollinators and pushing their roots into the clay soil that we tend to find unforgiving, but these native plants need to thrive. Each day for a month, in the late afternoon I startle a young rabbit who's feasting on the fescue lawn I've ignored—it lets me plant within just a few feet before running off into the shrubs. At night, lying in bed when

I can't fall asleep, I busy my mind with thoughts of the landscape.
I don't count sheep, I count plants—what was added, what could
be added, what was lost. I imagine short grasses supporting taller
wildflowers, roots touching and talking and helping one another;
I imagine larvae eating leaves and heading for the thick shelter
of switchgrass to pupate; I imagine birds scraping at the covered
ground for seeds, so loud you'd think they were mountain lions
pouncing on their prey.

I took away another 150 feet of lawn to make room for a gravel
patio where I can sit and watch the young meadow evolve; now, in
total, our quarter-acre lot might have 500 to 750 feet of lawn left—
I can mow it in ten minutes and get back to being in the garden. In
midsummer, from the deck I hear dozens of bumble bees working
wild senna, buzzing their bodies to shake the pollen loose. In early
fall, I can smell zigzag goldenrod from across the beds, a scent
that's the spitting image of my late grandmother's perfume.

Winter is coming tomorrow night after a long, dry fall. It's No-
vember 16 and the temperature is 80, the latest 80-degree day in
recorded history for the city. In two days it will be 42 degrees with
wind chills in the low 20s. I will miss having the windows open
and the cardinal's voice flooding the house as it chips away at twilight; I will miss letting our cats out as I plant the new gardens
and they sun themselves in the young grasses; I will miss the very
late sulphurs scrambling to find faded blooms long since absent of
nectar; and I will miss the grasshoppers who, in the still heat of a
June-like afternoon near Thanksgiving, jump loudly from leaf pile
to leaf pile and whose world may be growing larger in this small
suburban island that I now leave to them.

It's time to rethink beauty, to reimagine our gardens and urban
landscapes as we move into an uncertain future. Our gardens matter not because they can literally save species, but because they
are a call to action to be more than we let ourselves be. Gardens
are living testaments to our wonder and joy, our part of the larger

world and participation with all life. Gardens matter because they bring birds and butterflies closer to us, they help release endorphins that make us feel happy, awaken dormant connections in our neurons, maybe even spur empathy as we learn again to care selflessly for other species simply because it's the right or ethical thing to do. Gardens matter because they call us to act on issues of social justice, bringing nature and opportunity to those humans and other species who are marginalized by our culture. Gardens move us out from ourselves into a community of selves that depend upon and celebrate one another.

When we learn what our landscapes can do, how they can directly help wildlife and serve as ethical symbols for people—when we learn how essential native plants are, how gardens can sequester carbon and provide pollen and serve as larval hosts and rebuild our homes—then the choices we make after these revelations carry even more weight. Do we choose to garden for ourselves only, for our idea of beauty alone, or do we more fully—more equally—integrate a selfless gardening that builds ecosystems composed of essential native plants and designs that mimic the natural, wilder areas just beyond the garden fence? Or do we embrace our role as an indifferent species, a species bent on emotional and physical conquest that will undermine our health, happiness, and peace in the years to come?

Does a large home need all that grass and boxwood parterres? Does that style fit the regional environment aesthetically and ecologically? What happens when we go against the ecological grain of our home places, when we can't or won't accept the natural processes, beauty, and purpose of our immediate world? What happens to a species that sees landscapes as never quite right, never perfect enough, not entirely what we want? Does that species lose any right to be part of the larger world, does it lose its identity and potential to be something better?

Our gardens matter, and the way in which we create them, grow them, and rethink them matters on a level far more important than whether they simply function aesthetically. While we arguably must find a garden beautiful, and while it will always be a kind of artifice, the truth is the entire world is now a garden we have made. How we tend it, how we honor those species we've ignored and betrayed, will say much about who we are and who we will become. Our legacy won't be how pretty our gardens looked; our legacy will be how gardens and other managed spaces woke us to a revolution of belonging in this world, a renaissance of ethical thinking that helped us evolve into our fullest potential as stewards of life and gardeners of our own hearts.

In the spirit of an evolved landscape community, here is a new garden ethic for this century.

Your garden is a protest. It is a place of defiant compassion. It is a space to help sustain wildlife and ecosystem function while providing an aesthetic response that moves you. For you, beauty isn't just petal deep, but goes down into the soil, farther down into the aquifer, and back up into the air and for miles around on the backs and legs of insects. You don't have to see soil microbes in action, birds eating seeds, butterflies laying eggs, ants farming aphids—just knowing it's possible in your garden thrills you. It's like faith, and it frees you to live life more authentically. Your garden is a protest for all the ways in which we deny our life by denying other lives. Plant some natives. Be defiantly compassionate.

CHAPTER 2

More Than Native Plants

All through Taoist thought, there is the idea that our
disasters come from letting nothing live for itself,
from the longing we have to pull everything, even
friends, in to ourselves and let nothing alone. If we
examine a pine carefully, we see how independent
it is of us. When we first sense that a pine tree
really doesn't need us, that it has a physical life
and a moral life and a spiritual life that is complete
without us, we feel alienated and depressed.
The second time we feel it, we feel joyful.

—ROBERT BLY

A FEW WEEKS AFTER I turned ten years old, my parents moved
the family from Oklahoma to Minnesota. I can't begin to
convey how abrupt the change in environment was. Imagine
having lived your entire life with one parent in the Mojave Desert
only to wake up one day with a family of ten in a downtown New
York apartment. For me, Oklahoma was wind and heat, a flatness
of winter wheat, and the ability to watch the Sun set over the horizon. Oklahoma was devoid of what most would call nature. In
many ways, and for a long time, I despised it and the rural small-
town atmosphere I came from.

Minnesota was woods, even among the endless tracts of suburban houses; it was lakes and rivers, squirrels and birds, and

dampness and darkness, not to mention unending traffic and places to shop. One of the more visceral early moments after the move was exploring a pocket of conifers and maples a block down the street from our rental duplex that first autumn. Between two houses you could slide into a wider expanse of forest, even if that forest was only one or two lot sizes. I remember the softness of the woodland floor piled with pine needles, the way stabs of sunlight broke through the muffled leaves above and appeared almost foggy and diffuse. The scent was rich and moist, like a cellar lined in cedar planks. Totally out of my element, I felt for the first time in my life what I'd feel from then on when I walked into a wilder area—a complex mix of dread, euphoria, confusion, loss, and primal discovery.

I imagine kneeling down in that place now, warm in the light and cold in the shadows of rough tree trunks. My knees quickly become wet as I reach for a pinecone; I can perfectly fit the tips of my fingers between its smooth blades. What I'm sure of, what I'll remember clearly for the rest of my life, is being startled by a group of large Canada geese that quickly skimmed the treetops. At the time, I had no idea what they were. Their calls were upon me so suddenly I arched my back a bit, cowered as if anticipating a hawk's talons in my flesh. Those geese were so loud and yet so soft—I could hear not only their sharp voices but the push and pull of their wings against the air. It was the sound of someone putting on a jacket ready to enter the unknown.

Wherever I am today and a flock flies overhead, I know I am being blessed. I'm being gathered into the fold of the world, my experiences with nature at home and in places like the Boundary Waters or Nebraska Sandhills linked to one another—not just as one constant memory building upon itself, but as a lesson being passed down, another word in a sentence. Despite these experiences, more often than not I, like many people, am far removed from daily moments in the natural world. When I was ten maybe, I carried that pinecone home and put it on my dresser top to keep the raw feeling of a place with me as long as I could, stoking the embers that echo in me even now. When did we stop walking in the woods? When did we stop placing found objects on our dresser tops? When did we lose our simple, joyous wonder and humility? How do we reawaken the impulse to trust the life around us—life that has always been here?

Do we know what nature is in the context of our lives? I'm not entirely sure what it is in mine. I may have a garden, I may walk a prairie with my wife on occasion, I may be able to quote the weather forecast verbatim, but I don't think I'm part of the natural world in a meaningful sense. Historian William Cronon believes that nature is "the meeting place between the world 'out there' and the culturally constructed ideas and beliefs and values we project onto that world." Perhaps nature defies definition because we each live it so differently, our experiences and traditions coloring in what a place or a moment means. And yet we form similar opinions, bonds of expression, when we look out at a mountain or a lake in autumn and whisper to one another, "Isn't that beautiful," or, "I'm so happy you're here with me."

Landscape philosopher John Dixon Hunt, in his book *Greater Perfections: The Practice of Garden Theory*, says there are three natures. The first is wild, undisturbed, and unseen landscapes, which aren't likely to exist anymore but that we try to create or preserve in national parks and wildlife refuges. The second nature is agriculture, cities, and man-made geographic features like the Nazca lines in Peru. The third and final nature is gardens—that place where we attempt to artistically recreate what we emotionally feel and culturally perceive in the world around us. It's this third nature which provides us the most fertile ground for debate; if humans are nature and are thus natural, then every act we perform in reshaping the world is in essence landscape design. These acts include not only restoration but destruction. If gardens are a celebratory art form more than they are a utilitarian or profit-driven interference, then are they always natural? Are they always

of nature? Are they always worth celebrating? Are gardens somehow like the artistic display of male bower birds, who gather and
carefully arrange found objects like sticks, stones, berries, and even
trash to appeal to a female?

I'm less and less certain what nature is in the context of our
reshaping it, and have come to believe that trying to define it is
both useful and detrimental. Humans have a tendency, perhaps a
primal need, to categorize and organize our world, probably as a
way to make sense of it. But are we really part of this wild design,
or outside of it? Are we part of an evolutionary or divine purpose
as we remake the world in cities and farms and gardens? The act
of asking these questions is part of balancing life. Maybe the only
definition of nature we need is soil under our fingernails or recognizing the call of an unseen nuthatch.

For a long time, caterpillars that ate our leaves or bees that buzzed
our patio dinners were seen as enemies—and for many they
are still pests to be sprayed away. And yet our awareness of the
purpose, design, and deeper beauty of these creatures is helping
gardens evolve. As we realize how threatened wildness is, as we
redefine what nature is in our everyday lives in Western culture,
gardeners have come to the benefits of native plants and a bour-
geoning awareness of what role they play for us and other species,
in both scientific and philosophical ways. Gardeners have always
approached their practice with a mixture of humbleness and superiority—which is probably necessary for any successful art or
human endeavor. Running through the act of gardening with
native plants is the idea that gardeners seek a more biocentric
existence, one in which all species are equal, instead of an anthro-
pocentric existence in which human concerns and perspectives are
paramount. Gardens can be an important guide toward bringing
us more fully into life—and life more fully into us.

Before we delve into the ways that native plants are crucial for
our landscapes, and the complex cultural issues they bring up,

it's essential to define what they are. For some, native plants are those that were not brought to North America by humans at any point in time, while for others, even plants imported hundreds of years ago may now be considered native.[1] In their book *The Living Landscape*, Doug Tallamy and Rick Darke take a stab at defining the often-controversial term; they say a native is "a plant that has evolved in a given place over a period of time sufficient to develop complex and essential relationships with the physical environment and other organisms in a given ecological community." I favor this definition even while it's open to fine-tuning; the trickiest word in it, though, might be *evolved*, because evolution comes in a plethora of flavors over various time frames. While for the vast majority of organisms, coevolution between species takes thousands or even tens of thousands of years, there's evidence that some faster, human-caused evolution is also at play. For instance, cliff swallows who build their nests underneath bridge overpasses on I-80 in Nebraska have evolved smaller wings in the last half century to more quickly dodge traffic; weeds in Paris now produce heavier seeds to drop back into the same concrete cracks from which their parent sprouted; and over the past decades, fewer African elephants are developing tusks, as adults are poached for their ivory, making them unable to pass on the necessary genes for growing tusks. Every day we are causing accelerated or forced adaptation and evolution, and we do that in our landscape choices too, as we mix plants from around the world and create new interactions between flora and fauna.

While definitions of what makes a plant native vary based on belief and profession, I define native plants as preindustrial revolution—that is, plants in a given environment that were present, and part of the functioning ecology and biodiversity, before Western civilization plowed them up and/or altered the chemistry of the atmosphere with exhaust from fossil fuels. Some go back further, especially in the context of North America, and pinpoint ten thousand years ago at the dawn of human agriculture and the hunting to extinction of big game like mammoths and saber-toothed tigers. Others, to be sarcastically argumentative, will reach even further back in time when the continents were one land mass—or when the first asteroids brought microbes and ice crashing onto our molten world. Regardless of the time frame, nearly all experts believe native plants are important, not only to the spirit of a place but also to its wildlife and ecology.

Despite the importance of native plants, a common refrain in response to how or why we should use them is offered by Adrian Higgins. In his review of Thomas Rainer and Claudia West's transformative book *Planting in a Post-Wild World*, Higgins says: "They [Rainer and West] reject the popular approach of using indigenous plants exclusively to redeem wilderness because such a place no longer exists." In other words, using a majority of native plants, particularly in the context of highly altered places like cities and industrial agriculture, will not recreate, stabilize, or be of significant ecological benefit because the historical wildness or ecosystem no longer exists. On the surface, the argument seems logical, but looking more deeply we can see it's problematic on many levels; addressing the statement's limitations is at the heart of this book.

In the pages ahead, it's my goal to show the following: First, that native plant garden design is not about redeeming wilderness, as suggested by Higgins and many others, but reviving it. While wilderness may not exist in the bucolically pristine way we culturally idealize it in art and film, the ecological interactions and especially the species that depend on wildness—and native plants—are still very much here and critically important to our future, even if the original native landscape is gone forever. Second, realizing these facts, native plants should constitute a significant majority in our landscapes, and in fact can comprise nearly 100 percent of our gardens. We don't have to lose beauty or function; from phytoremediation to insect reproduction to stabilizing songbird populations to human-created aesthetics, native plants are as crucial in the urban and suburban environment as they are "in the wild." In other words, there is a native plant for most any situation, and

in the case of pollinators—who some studies show are now pre-
ferring urban habitats due to floral abundance—the wildlife are
hungry and waiting.

About a month before my wife and I were married in 2007, we
began building the garden at our new home. I remember saying
that I wanted a garden, but neither one of us understood exactly
what that meant—or how crazy it would become when we started
spreading 17 cubic yards of wood mulch by bucket and wheel-
barrow in the brutal July heat. Those first garden beds comprised
about 1,800 square feet, with most of the area being a large space
on the southwest corner of our quarter-acre suburban lot. About
half of the lots in our development didn't yet have houses, and our
lawn wasn't even in, but our departure from the suburban norm
had fully begun.

As I plotted and planted the garden, I spent six to eight hours
a day outside several times a week, and on one trip to a nursery,
racked up a thousand-dollar bill. When choosing shrubs and
flowers, I went solely by the plant tags in those days, at first
agonizing over the radically different areas of bone-dry or mucky
clay, as well as figuring well, sure, it'd be neat to see butterflies. So
I started noting plant tags with butterfly symbols. One such plant
was swamp milkweed.

It wasn't long after I wrestled the milkweed into the soil that I
saw fat yellow, black, and white striped caterpillars on the leaves,
or what was left of the leaves. I was angry that these apparent pests
were destroying a ten-dollar plant, and certainly wasn't going to
stand for it. I had already amassed a collection of fertilizers and
insecticides in the garage, as any "good" gardener does, and halfway
back to the milkweed with spray in hand, I stopped in my tracks.
Shouldn't I first research what those caterpillars are? Wasn't I the
least bit curious? Turns out they were monarch larvae who would
transform into the large, blazing blurs of orange that symbolize
healthy gardens.

That's when, so early on, I slowly began to shift away from how my mother and my culture had taught me to garden—and who to garden for. Back then monarch butterfly and pollinator issues weren't nearly as prevalent in the news as they are today, and it was still a year or more before I knew anything about their migration and population struggles. But for the first time, I began to seriously question my plants and my garden. I didn't just consider what the plants looked like or if they'd grow, but also how they'd act and who they'd support in the garden.

It may be that, like other power-driven systems such as agriculture and bioengineering, our gardening culture too often seeks to control and interpret nature, instead of helping us be a more integrated, humble, and functioning part of natural processes. While I admit my own landscape is very much for me, a space I define and create and that serves my aesthetic and ethical beliefs as any garden does, I've tried to navigate a culture that isn't just mine—a culture of other species and a nature we share together, a combined culture of reciprocity and understanding. There are plenty of times when I avoid walking down a path so as not to disturb a bird, butterfly, or frog, and I'm constantly leaving a spent bloom or broken twig when I see wildlife using it. I find it increasingly hard to be a part of my garden as it matures because I am, in essence, giving much of it away. I feel like I'm losing ownership, entitlement, and the right to make alterations as I observe how the landscape is being used. Ultimately, I've come to realize, it's liberating to find myself among these unfamiliar sensations. The less I "garden," the more I become a part of something larger than the garden.

In *The Spell of The Sensuous*, author David Abram explores what nature means in the modern, human-dominated world.

> As technological civilization diminishes the biotic diversity of the earth, language itself is diminished. As there are fewer and fewer songbirds in the air, due to the destruction

of their forests and wetlands, human speech loses more and more of its evocative power. When we no longer hear the voices of warbler and wren, our own speaking can no longer be nourished by their cadences. As the splashing speech of the rivers is silenced by more and more dams, as we drive more and more of the land's wild voices into the oblivion of extinction, our own languages become increasingly impoverished and weightless, progressively emptied of their earthly resonance.

Abram's thoughts, though not specifically about native plants, are an entry point into exploring the complications and importance of wildlife gardening with such flora. For Abram, if not all of us, there's a subtle and growing absence of shared language, perspective, and community. Native plants, and gardens created with a much more pronounced purpose for other species, challenge a plethora of cultural and social conceptions of nature and our place in it. The native plant discussion forces us to think about landscapes with a deeper purpose, and especially asks us to consider lives and voices other than our own. When we ask what a plant's purpose is besides looking pretty, it can be easy to feel like our plant choices—and even how we live our lives—are being called into question. And it's easy to become defensive wondering why folks don't just mind their own business, or stop asking why plants have to do more than look pretty.

When we start asking this last question, we complicate what was a simple, feel-good moment of walking into a nursery and finding love at first sight. When we ask a plant to feed caterpillars and butterflies and birds and spiders, as well as help add soil fertility or sequester carbon from the air, we're opening a whole can of worms. We begin to doubt ourselves and our society's role in the environment. Heck, even the word "environment" is now saturated with animosity, being hijacked by politics to create doubt and fear so those in power can keep their control. As terms like "environmentalist" have become loaded, often implying that science is more opinion or ideology than fact, so too have other words like "native plants." But exploring the natural and social science will help us define native plants in a time of estrangement from nature, and help us glimpse how that estrangement is holding us back.

We can see native plants not as an indictment, a stumbling block, or something that undermines our existence. Instead, we can use them as a catalyst to more fully explore our role in human and other natural communities, and to critically engage with what it means to so thoroughly shape individual species and entire ecosystems. In what ways do the plants we choose reflect our values and knowledge? In what ways do our private and public landscapes determine our future cultural and social policies? How do intimate spaces we delicately and purposefully manage at home either affirm or call into question our relationships with life beyond the garden?

For many, such an exploration will feel uncomfortable for a variety of reasons. Any discussion about gardens comes right into our personal lives and our personal property—it feels like an invasion of our rights or freedom. Couple that with the intimate and subjective process of reading, and it's nearly impossible not to feel attacked or criticized, or in the very least exposed and vulnerable. These feelings are all incredibly valid and valuable on this journey. When our assumptions are tested, our first response will often be an uncomfortable revulsion, but that response is the first step toward thinking more openly and honestly about who we are and who we want to be. It's not easy and it shouldn't be. For me, the native plant conversation is not one of resistance or a hard-line fundamentalist stance. Instead, the conversation is about stoking the embers of connectivity to the natural world while reimagining and recreating a human culture that values other cultures (plant and animal) as much as its own. Such empathy and compassion does not come easily to us, even among ourselves.

I make it a point to stroll my gardens—now approaching 5,000 square feet—several times a day. One evening when I came back inside from one of these strolls, I grabbed a plate of cookies and collapsed on the couch. About half an hour into a *Mythbusters* episode on duct tape survival tactics, I glanced down to see a large black leaf or clod of dirt slowly climbing my jeans. It was a bumble bee. After a few seconds of alarm, I lurched forward, my beating chest hunched over my knees, waiting for the painful prick of a stinger to slice through the denim. The moment was very much like my recurring childhood nightmare where the statue of a medieval knight in the basement came to life, made its way up two flights of stairs, stood in my doorway making sure I was asleep, then crept toward my bed raising an ax. I would always pull the sheet over my face, close my eyes, and hold as still as stone until I was sure the knight had left. But now, with the bumble bee making its way up my leg, instead of running for the door or assuming I was about to be in pain, I leaned back into the couch cushions and began to process my fear. I held as still as possible.

Thinking the moment through, I reminded myself that I'd never been stung in the garden, not even when my nose was smelling a flower two inches away from bees gathering pollen on another bloom. I then recalled one of my early landscape design consultations where a father asked for flowers that didn't attract bees along the front sidewalk, for the sake of his children. Suddenly, this experience in my living room made more sense. While it's normal to want to protect ourselves and our family from dangers in nature, we can easily let our fears take us too far. My fear was unfounded. I'd heard stories of folks picking up bumble bees on cool autumn mornings and placing them in the sun; there, the bees would warm up and then fly away. I read how only females could sting, and perhaps I had a male on me. So I got up, walked outside, gently pinched the bee between two fingers, and put it on the leaves of a culver's root. In that brief moment of touching this creature, another wall was broken down between my culture and the other cultures of the world we marginalize, brutalize, and misunderstand.

Over the last forty years, global invertebrate numbers, of which insects are a part, have declined 45 percent. In that same time frame, butterflies and moths have declined 35 percent. And these facts go even deeper into the ecosystem. Ninety-six percent of songbirds—those we have the most contact with in our daily lives—have young that can only eat insects, and 90 percent of these insect species can only feed on native plants. In fact, native plants sustain 35 times the biomass of caterpillars compared to non-native plants. Of the approximately 93 butterfly species in California—a botanically rich and diverse state—65 species can only reproduce on native plants. It's clear that without native plants, insect and bird populations will continue to be threatened.

The base of the food chain, insects, are still very much among us. Even if the native, preindustrial ecosystems are gone in many areas, the interactions for a large portion of the fauna still exist. Tiger swallowtails seek out green ash, black cherry, and American plum for egg laying, and late-summer nesting goldfinches specifically use thistle fluff to line their nests. We've pushed wildlife to the margins of our lives, not only metaphysically, through our fear and desires, but physically in urban, suburban, and industrial agriculture—not to mention climate disruption that's forcing species to adapt, move, or die.

If we go back to birds, especially those charismatic, canopy-dwelling species like cardinals and woodpeckers that are part of our daily lives, we can look to a study that explores bird diversity in suburban landscapes. The authors—Karin Burghardt, Doug Tallamy, and Gregory Shriver—analyzed the abundance and number of bird and caterpillar species in six pairs of suburban gardens. The landscapes in each pair were of comparable size and plant cover, one composed entirely of native plants, the other with a mix of native and exotic. The results in this moderate sample size in one region (the northeast) showed that the all-native landscapes supported eight times the number of caterpillars, birds, and bird species of conservation concern. Clearly native plants, even in a radically altered suburban setting, positively affect the abundance and biodiversity of native wildlife.

Often, the argument goes that being a native plant "purist"—a relatively polite though pejorative term—makes the perfect the enemy of the good; having a 100 percent or even 75 percent native plant landscape is not only functionally unrealistic but also unfair to humans because it's limiting, constrictive, and otherwise undemocratic. In other words, a native plant garden reduces human freedom and maybe isn't as necessary for supporting animal biodiversity. None of these tenets are true unless we're gardening for just one species. If, on the other hand, our intent is to garden for the community, then native plants are not limiting but in fact give life and freedom to countless seen and unseen fauna above and below the soil line. It may also be that the biotic redundancy and ecological health that native plants tend to foster will also impact the stability of our own health, even our own cultural systems that flourish atop thriving and functioning biodiversity. Our modern good fortune—our food, shelter, longevity, and even technology—rests squarely on the ecological redundancies and immense biodiversity we've luckily found ourselves among.

With climate zones moving north and uphill at a rate of 3.8 feet per day, the options for wildlife and even plants to adapt are dwindling. Time is not on their side. The very least we can do is provide an opportunity, a small chance, for adaptation through evolution and/or migration to occur. Ground and canopy birds are appearing north of their usual ranges, and even flowers are moving up hills and mountainsides as they follow their evolved niches. Our four thousand species of native bees may be especially at risk, particularly larger bees like bumble bees who evolved in a cooler climate and those with shorter flight times that coincide with changing bloom cycles. Within those blooms is highly nutritious pollen, which bees use to feed their young. One of the most beneficial groups of plants for bees and other pollinators is goldenrod, which from 1842 to 2014 has seen a reduction in pollen protein content of 30 percent. Such loss is due to elevated levels of CO_2 in the atmosphere and will not only affect bee health but also bee size, which in turn affects a bee's ability to successfully forage. As plants produce more carbohydrates in response to increased carbon in the air, essential nutrients like zinc, iron, and vitamin A become diluted, making plants less nutritious for humans and insects alike.

If we look even closer at bees and other pollinators, their exposure to environmental pressures should make us think twice about how we garden—and why we garden—in our backyards, public parks, industrial campuses, roadsides, and more. Eighty-seven percent of the world's flowering plants, including most of our primary food crops, require insects to reproduce. A healthy minority of those flowering plants have some degree of specialist relationship with native bees—meaning that a native bee times its emergence from the nest to coincide with a specific plant's bloom. Without that one bee species, the flower may not set seed or have as many high-quality seeds with healthy genetics. Even the loss of just one specialist bee species can send an entire ecosystem out of whack, prompting other bees to become less-efficient generalists.

Research by Berry Brosi and Heather Briggs shows that the loss of just one bumble bee species leads to wildflower seed production declines of one-third. Their work bears out how floral fidelity—the phenomenon by which bees visit only one species at a time while it's in bloom—benefits plants in significant ways. Brosi and Briggs found that, "when bees are promiscuous, visiting plants of more than one species during a single foraging session, they are much less effective as pollinators." Bumble bees are critical pollinators, able to muscle into closed flowers like blue wild indigo, turtlehead, and gentian, while also performing buzz pollination; these bees may deliver fifteen to twenty pollen grains each time they visit a flower, which compares to only three to four grains on honey bees. In fact, two hundred and fifty native orchard mason bees can pollinate an entire acre of apple trees, whereas fifteen to twenty thousand honey bees, trucked in from half a country away and under incredible stress, are needed to do the same job at great expense. Further, bumble bees are active in colder weather—this is why you'll often see them hard at work in a light summer rain shower or on cool fall afternoons.

What does this all have to do with native plants? Native bees are more efficient pollinators, having a 91 to 72 percent advantage over honey bees. Flower diversity and seed set is lower with their absence. Native bees have coevolved relationships with many flowers, and those flowers in turn play ecological roles in their wild and revived niches. Of the 450 native bee species endemic to the mid-Atlantic and New England region, one-third are pollen specialists relying on a specific genus or even species to feed their young. And while specialist bees make up only 20 percent of the entire bee population, their presence indicates higher-quality habitat. If you're into attractive fruit, as most consumers are, you'll want specialist bees and other pollinators in great numbers. Fifty percent of our produce is left in the field or thrown away because it doesn't look good; but when strawberries are pollinated by a large diversity of bees, they are firmer, redder, and have a longer shelf life.

We've been duped by "save the bee" campaigns that show images of European honey bees or graphics of honeycomb.[2] We don't really need honey bees in North America for pollination. The primary group that needs honey bees is an industrial agriculture system that has come to depend upon them; this insect species is one more cog in the industrialization of life that minimizes and destroys ecosystems for profit. We put great stress on these bees, shipping them around the nation, treating them like machine parts with dollar values as their primary worth. Worse, honey bees outcompete native bees for forage—which in turn will alter the appearance and function of an ecosystem over time. Researchers from Lund University in Sweden placed hives in various areas and discovered that where those hives appeared, bumble bees vanished almost entirely. Couple this competition with the fact that honey bees are more prone to carrying viral diseases that can spread to other species, and then we have much larger problems.

A similar study by Sheila Colla and Scott MacIvor definitively shows how honey bees outcompete native bees and are not even a global conservation threat. Native bees active at the end of the summer—keep in mind most species have flight times of just a few weeks—were the most affected by the presence of honey bees, who are more abundant and can easily outforage specialists. Additionally, honey bees can enhance invasive plant seed production—particularly since they evolved with these introduced plants, which are commonly from Eurasia—and these plants, when in bloom, can distract native bees from their native plant relationships. Often we hear about helping bees by using any type of flowering plant that extends or heightens the bloom season; perhaps we're doing as much if not more harm by using non-natives, especially when they may perform fewer ecosystem services overall. Even if some native bees are foraging meaningfully on exotics, honey bees that likely coevolved with those exotic plants might out-forage those generalist native bee species. Unfortunately, suburban and urban environments not only lack the native plants so many pollinators need to thrive, but the air itself can hinder their ability to find flowers. Smog destroys floral scents, as bees in urban areas with higher air pollution can find flowers only 35 percent of the time. For the many small bees that can only travel up to three blocks before needing to refuel, the lack of usable blooms in good quantity is compounded by the increase in pollution.

The immense diversity of pollinators our native plants support is incredible, especially the adults that come to forage for nectar and pollen. While it's critical we track these interactions regionally and even locally over decades and centuries, we can look to one person to get a glimpse into the complex social sphere of some natives. From 1880 to 1910, entomologist Charles Robertson catalogued insect species visiting prairie wildflowers in a ten-mile radius around Carlinville in southwest Illinois. While surely Robertson's environment held a greater abundance of prairie at the time, not to mention a likely greater abundance and diversity of insects, we can see how his results show the historic impact of wildflowers on pollinators. He found that New England aster attracted 82 species of adult pollinator, common boneset 191, wild bergamot 131, purple prairie clover 134, rattlesnake master 187, Virginia mountain mint 130, gray-headed coneflower 130, black-eyed Susan 201, stiff goldenrod 121, and golden Alexanders 209. These plant species run almost the full gamut of the growing season from April to September, creating a nice bloom succession. And coupled with the hundreds of other endemic plant species—including shrubs, trees, grasses, and sedges—these common forbs would provide everything a growing bee or moth might need, not to mention the innumerable ecosystem services plant communities foster. What role might the plants in Robertson's catalog play in our modern urban landscape? Even if that role is not up to a historical benchmark, they are still critically important to the evolving environment and the wildlife within it.

This all might seem overwhelming. We didn't create these environmental problems on purpose or with all the facts in hand. Looking at our personal lives—how we directly interact with the world around us—is only a drop in the bucket. And yet, with enough drops we have gallons. Humans are especially able to adapt through critical thinking and reflection; we aren't the only ones to do so, but we are the primary species that so quickly and radically alters our environment on such a large scale. This is why we need more examples of native plant communities in areas we drive by every day, including outside office windows, schoolroom windows, and even prison windows.

If kids today see 35 percent fewer butterflies than did their parent's generation, how do these kids know or feel that loss? They can't. They simply come to know the loss as normal. Eventually, hearing only blue jays while sipping our morning tea on the back porch may be normal—no wrens or chickadees or finches or doves or flickers. As for most of us, the days after 9/11 are seared into my memory, and one of the most visceral experiences was the total silence in the skies above. No jets, no helicopters, no contrails, and yet how normal it soon became, how absence defined us and our struggles.

Without native plants, our world faces mass silence on a scale that's overwhelming, unfathomable, and maybe even unknowable. We've identified only a fraction of the species that make our world function. In another twist, native plants are not always as native as they seem—at least not when it comes to making them available via the nursery trade, where yet another industrialization of life is taking place that both benefits and harms our world. The pressure to create new plants, to make new plants available for a marketplace, is extensive—not only those plants found in the wild, but those bred for certain physical traits that are appealing to us. Yet something can be left behind when we alter plants or produce them in ways contrary to natural environments—namely, ecosystem function and even resilience in the face of changing climates.

The University of Delaware and the Mt. Cuba Center are exploring how insects use native plants and native plant cultivars in the northeast. Cultivars can arise in several ways: from a wild selection or a sport found in a garden; a plant bred for specific traits, often a hybrid between two species; or genetic engineering, where DNA is altered to produce a desired trait (the latter is often far too expensive for ornamental garden plants). While the UD/Mt. Cuba analysis is limited by plant species and region, it gives us a glimpse into issues that need to be further studied around the country as they raise crucial concerns.

As researchers at Mt. Cuba explored how different traits affect a plant's palatability to caterpillars, a few aspects became clear: cultivars bred to have purple leaves are far less attractive to insect larvae as compared to wild or straight species with green leaves. This is probably due to higher levels of anthocyanins, chemicals that deter insect feeding. Other cultivars (like chandler highbush blueberry) have been bred to have larger or abundant fruits, and these actually appeared to be more attractive to caterpillars. Changes in size or habit—for example, plants that grow more compactly or taller than the straight species—do not seem to influence caterpillar feeding, nor does breeding for disease resistance, as with the Princeton elm. However, these results are local, and they only look at insects feeding on leaves—not adult pollinators or a plethora of other ecological services in the larger community. Some ongoing early-stage studies will gauge nectar and pollen nutrition in native plant cultivars compared to straight species. So far, the numbers are showing a fifty/fifty split between attractiveness of blooms to pollinators. However, those results do not go into the details of nectar and pollen composition, so the reasons for pollinator interaction may have to do with flower color or shape, as well as other extrasensory cues like ultraviolet markers on petals.

There are additional issues at play regarding native plant cultivars, and these deserve more careful thought. Most cultivars are produced asexually as clones; this preserves the desirable traits such as leaf color, flower shape, and specimen form. That preservation is what makes the plants a boon. Nurseries know what they're getting, designers know what they're getting, and customers know what they're getting: something predictable and familiar. It makes selling the product far easier. But at the same time, filling landscapes with the same plant—literally the same plant—opens up the possibility of mass die-offs from diseases, predators, and the like, as well as a reduction in genetic diversity and the consequent ability of multiple wildlife species to use the plants.

These last two points get to the heart of the matter. The holy grail of native plants is using local genotype or ecotype seed—seed from plants originating within a specific radius, often a hundred or fifty miles (or less), and seed responsibly collected from wild, remnant populations. Using local ecotype plants means they are even more adapted to local conditions, which could in turn make them more resistant to specific environmental extremes, predators, or diseases. But these plants must be produced through open pollination, which means that the offspring—while genetically similar to the parent—can also be physically very different. Such variability is not prized in the horticulture trade, and to educate a consumer on this fact requires doing almost a 180-degree turn on our expectations when walking into a nursery. For many consumers, buying a plant that's not in bloom or doesn't look perfect in shape is unthinkable.

We know that when we homogenize environments bad things happen. We can look to corn and soybean fields as an example, where one plant is given privilege over all others, but we can also see it in horticulture. Dutch elm disease comes to mind, where we lost entire streets of trees—just as we will with the ash and the emerald ash borer. Research that explored common nursery plants for sale in several large metro areas around the country showed the plants in those cities were more genetically similar to each other than they were to plants in wild populations just outside the city limits. When plants in Atlanta gardens are the same as plants in Minneapolis gardens, we're setting up not only gardeners for failure, but also pollinators and the plants themselves.

Many native plant cultivars will resume the open-pollination processes of straight species plants, and those new plants will often revert to characteristics of the straight species. But will their bloom time be in sync with local pollinators? What about interactions with soil organisms and other plants in the community? Local ecotype plants are the gold standard; they have the genetic traits to thrive in the local environment, and should limit genetic diversity to those best-adapted traits. The argument for mixing exotics and native cultivars in with straight species is at the most obvious and basic level highly problematic and not nearly studied enough. Even the common suggestion to include non-native plants in order to increase the seasonal availability of blooms is suspect; by adding non-native flowering plants, are we altering the forage competition and composition of key pollinators like bees? What larvae are these non-native plants supporting? How are the plants contributing beyond the aesthetic and management-driven functionality of the space, increasing and reviving local biodiversity?

And then what about adding native plants from nearby, warmer ecoregions to prepare or adapt the garden and any potential new wildlife for our changing weather patterns? In Chapter 4 we'll look at novel ecosystems and the impossibility of predicting when or if plants become invasive, which further complicates the discussion of our landscape choices.

So far the entire conversation here has focused on native plants in our gardens. But I want to go further, especially in the context of where I've spent most of my life—the Great Plains, the Midwest, the tallgrass prairie. My perspective is born from the echo of a unique and ecologically important environment—and it's my hope that, over time, your perspective on gardens and nature will come from a deeper look into your region, if it doesn't already.

I come from prairie—something I only realized (and accepted) in my thirties. My family settled the mixed grass prairie of western Oklahoma in the 1890s, and as an adult, I've landed in Nebraska— a place located precisely between my childhood homes to the north and south. Nebraska has more distinct ecoregions within its borders than the entire region from its eastern edge to the Atlantic Ocean. The western shortgrass, rocky escarpments, and pine ridge give way to sandhill prairie and pothole ponds, to mixed grass prairies, wooded rivers, saline wetlands, oak savanna, and tallgrass prairie. For me, no conversation about native plants or gardens is complete without exploring prairie and North American grass-lands, of which up to 70 percent are on track to disappear by the end of the century. It's not flyover country—it's fly-into country for countless migrating birds and resident insects.

I don't recall the first time I stood on a prairie, and really, to "stand on a prairie" means you're on a small remnant where it's highly likely you can see a field of corn or houses off in the dis-tance. I'm fortunate to live within twenty minutes of three tallgrass remnants of several hundred acres each: Nine Mile Prairie, a virgin prairie used by the University of Nebraska for research; Pioneers

Park Prairie, the western edge of our largest municipal park; and Spring Creek Prairie, never tilled and still holding evidence of wheel ruts from a spur of the Oregon Trail. What vanishing local prairie remnants have taught me is that you can't walk a prairie once and call it a day, or even a season. Plants and wildlife are constantly shifting, hour by hour. To best absorb and understand a prairie, as with any place, you have to become intimate with it through many experiences—and you have to bring and leave with a vast array of honest, complicated emotions.

In fall the prairie is dipped in bronze, brown, and ochre. An hour before sunset, and the Sun is already creating halos around the thick seed heads of Indiangrass, while bees, skippers, and a few crescent butterflies find the last of the aromatic asters and Canada goldenrod hidden among short and tall bluestem turning crimson. Atop even a moderate hill, the air is warm from the day, but follow a path down a few dozen feet and an evening chill swarms my legs like grasshoppers disturbed from the vegetation. If I'm lucky there is silence—no cars on the nearby road, no planes on final approach for the airport, no gunshots from the nearby police shooting range. There is the riptide of grass in the wind rising against the horizon and the deep breath of getting down on my knees to admire a fringed gentian, so blue it's almost violet and giving birth to a bumble bee laden with pollen.

Sitting down among these tall grasses is a practice in making one's self small—and in many ways, a momentary part of a larger network of thought and resilience. Just below the surface, tens of thousands of miles of roots mingle and communicate; up to one-third of each grass's roots die every year, which enriches the soil by locking in sequestered carbon and other nutrients. A patch of big bluestem of one square yard has 130 feet of roots, and that same square yard one foot deep holds three to five million nematodes, which consume twice as much grass as a herd of cattle. One teaspoon of virgin prairie soil contains five billion microbes. Looking up I can almost imagine the bellies of horses, like those of the Spanish conquistador Coronado, who ventured as far as north-central Kansas, and whose men had to leave tall posts in order to find their way back to the southwest.

As a child in Minnesota, the forests seemed dangerous and dark. There was an equal measure of fear and exuberance, and I felt my breath escaping me as I looked for a way home. Here in the prairie—and maybe because I'm older—I only wish for more, millions of acres more to help me see what's coming over the horizon and prepare for the future. Grasslands used to cover one-third of the world, but tallgrass in America is now fragmented along with its wildlife, comprising only 1 to 2 percent of its original area. Since 2009 we've plowed up prairie the size of Kansas, 53 million acres, a rate faster than Amazon deforestation over the same time frame. That's also 3.2 billion metric tons of carbon released, equal to the exhaust emitted by 670 million cars. While I often meet people in awe of prairie and its plants, I don't tend to meet people who believe in it as something extremely valuable like a forest or a lake—something that should have a massive presence in our lives. It's hard to comprehend how, living in the "tallgrass" in eastern Nebraska, we so easily dismiss the place we profess to love. John Weaver, a great naturalist of the prairies, says this about tallgrass:

> The disappearance of a major natural unit of vegetation from the face of the earth is an event worthy of causing pause and consideration by any nation. Yet so gradually has the prairie been conquered by the breaking plow, the tractor, and the overcrowded herds of man... that scant attention has been given to the significance of this endless grassland or the course of its destruction. Civilized man is destroying a masterpiece of nature without recording for posterity that which he has destroyed.

That we can so rapidly and thoroughly erase an entire ecosystem of such size and complexity is suicidal. In fact, I'd argue it's murder if not genocide, because that's precisely what we're doing to places and the species that live there.

The most obvious and beloved symbol of prairie is the bison, a powerful and stunning animal whose numbers shrank from tens of millions to a few hundred over the course of several decades in the late 1800s. The largest land mammal in North America at the time wasn't hunted for sport or sustenance—it was hunted to subdue Native American Plains tribes whose entire culture revolved around its use. Once the animals were gone, the tribes would have no reason to be nomadic and would lose their primary food source, even aspects of their religion, and be forced to settle on reservations. Ultimately, for most of them, this meant confinement in Oklahoma, then confinement on acreages, which further broke up tribal and family units.

Ironically, it's Oklahoma where I've maybe best come to know prairie and its wildlife. I spent many years researching my family's genealogy and life in that place, as well as the state's cultural and geologic history. A place that I once loathed and was reluctant to return to became one of great respect and power for me—in no small measure thanks to a prairie dog colony.

Like bison, black-tailed prairie dogs once numbered in the tens of millions, perhaps hundreds of millions. One town would stretch across tens of thousands of acres, and just as it might take days for one bison herd to thunder by, it could take days for one person on horseback to leave a prairie dog colony. These small rodents are a keystone species, which means one to two hundred other prairie species depend on them or are in some way critically linked to them. Take burrowing owls, who use empty dens to raise their owlets; or golden eagles, who feed them to their young; or prairie rattlesnakes, northern grasshopper mice, jackrabbits, pronghorns, sagebrush lizards, ornate box turtles, and on and on. Prairie dogs also have a highly intelligent and complex language; in fact, it's so nuanced and accurate they can communicate to one another that "a tall human in a white shirt is coming from the south carrying a rifle."

I spent my early years less than an hour from the Wichita Mountains in west-central Oklahoma. Folks who actually live among mountains wouldn't call a 2,500-foot peak high, but these 540-million-year-old, granite-capped mountains are almost entirely buried under Rocky Mountain sediment and used to rival the tallest current landforms in the world. Looking out from Scott's Peak one can view the entire Wichita Mountains Wildlife Refuge, some 59,000 acres home to scissor-tailed flycatchers, Texas longhorns, bison, elk, and the last never-plowed vestiges of mixed grass prairie in the rocky terrain.

And of course there's a prairie dog colony.[3] Usually, prairie dogs are incredibly skittish and require a great deal of stillness and patience to witness. They'll make their "yip yip" calls, quickly scatter underground, and only begrudgingly poke their nose out from holes a good while later. Not so of the Wichita Mountains colony, who have become almost half-domesticated, accustomed to free snacks from tourists who stop in the parking lot to watch young ones scamper across the road and back.

Parents tumble with their offspring while keeping the ground of yellow-flowering basin sneezeweed neatly clipped to a height of only a few inches, which allows them a long, unobstructed view of potential predators—and which once attracted bison herds to the nutritious, fresh growth. I can stand in this place for hours. The prairie dog culture is at once so similar to our own and yet so different that I feel I can learn far more about the world and myself here than in any other place. The sharp, soft calls echo across the field within a valley, communications being made from a hundred yards away. Along the gravel access path, a dung beetle pushes its spherical load toward the colony.

In Nebraska, prairie dogs are nothing short of contentious. Where their numbers are higher, in western Nebraska, is where ranchland is the most prevalent; it's too dry to farm commodity crops. Prairie dogs are falsely blamed for the phenomenon of cattle slipping into holes and breaking legs, so they are poisoned en masse and left to bleed out internally over days and weeks, as are the predators who take advantage of the opportunity. Wherever we are, it seems, other life can't be—unless it's pretty, benign, and occasional. Every place we touch is a garden, no matter its size, and the economic, aesthetic, and emotional lessons we learn in one landscape are practiced in the others.

Our culture is a culture not of the land or of place, and not of understanding or equality. From 2011 to 2012, Nebraska led the nation in prairie conversion to row-crop agriculture to the tune of nearly 55,000 acres. Grassland nesting birds are declining much faster than any other group, and half of North America's ducks reproduce on the grasslands and prairie potholes of the central and northern Plains—precisely where conversion is happening the fastest.

A recent study in southern Wisconsin retraced the prairies that famed botanist and naturalist John Curtis studied in the late 1940s to mid-1950s. The new surveys show that the disappearance of species has tripled while the appearance of new, exotic species has doubled. Some sites have fewer than 18 percent of the originally documented species, and some are made up of 60 percent non-native species—which leads to one native plant species being lost each year, particularly specialist plants like rattlesnake master that give way to generalists. With the loss of biodiversity comes the loss of resilience as interactive communities, coevolved and performing niche services, become eradicated. If we can't know them in their wild setting, can we know them in their less wild urban gardens? What happens when we do know them again on a daily basis?

Such loss in prairie biodiversity from mismanaged landscapes and invasive exotics is just the tip of the compass plant. Our atmosphere now holds twice as much nitrogen and phosphorous as it did fifty years ago, primarily as a result of agricultural fertilization and fossil fuel use. The added nitrogen encourages grass to grow thicker and taller, which will crowd out other species like forbs. In bad years, during drought for example, the monoculture of grasses will naturally thin and grow shorter or go totally dormant, which will open up soil to more invasive plants and erosion.

A mature tallgrass prairie can absorb and filter nine inches of rain every hour. Wetlands found among such prairies are home to more than one third of all US endangered species. The world's grasslands hold one-third of all carbon stocks, almost as much as that stored by forests, and that carbon is held permanently in the soil until it's plowed up, whereas in a forest it is released as trees decay. In other words, a prairie can store more carbon below ground than a forest can above. Dr. Cynthia Camdardella, a soil scientist with the USDA's Agricultural Research Service National Laboratory for Agriculture and Environment, led a team that took four-foot soil core samples in the Neal Smith National Wildlife Refuge in central Iowa. The samples were taken from 19 reconstructed prairies ranging in age from one to 17 years old, in 2000, 2005, and 2010. As the prairies aged, the amount of biologically active carbon increased near the soil surface, due to fresh inputs of carbon from growing plants. Prairie age held no relation to how much carbon was stored in the soil, only to what was going on at the surface—the most active layer of soil building.

There's a reason so much corn, wheat, and soybeans are grown on the former prairies. And yet, we're discovering that active soil microbes—like those found in prairies—not only help store more carbon in the soil (50 to 80 percent more), but increase crop yields and pest resistance in plants. However, our dependence on chemicals like glyphosate destroys soil microbes, creating a dead soil that can't absorb water and in turn increases pollution of waterways through increased runoff.

Take for example Stephanie Strom's report from *The New York Times* showing that Iowa fields with biotech corn have hard, impermeable soils. When cornstalks were pulled up, a chunk of dirt they clung to came along; devoid of microbes, the soil was for all intents and purposes dead. Corn grown conventionally was more easily pulled up, and soil with a coffee-grounds texture fell off the more-developed roots. Glyphosate's big selling point is that it binds tightly to soil minerals, thus preventing chemical runoff, but this also means it competes with plants for the same mineral nutrients. Glyphosate can also alter the mix of bacteria and fungi, making plants more susceptible to parasites and pathogens, which requires additional inputs. The solution, Monsanto says, is to use soil mineral additives, which they would sell. The company is also moving into studying the production of microbes that can be added to soil. It could be argued, however, that crop rotation and cover crops could largely mitigate the need for such intensive inputs. We are plugging holes in a ship where we keep removing the rivets.

Topsoil is what's at stake in our remade world. It's scraped away in suburban development and washed away in rural fields. Global topsoil could be gone in sixty years or less—40 percent is already degraded or seriously degraded, leading to a reduction in food crop nutrients. In fact, topsoil is being lost at a rate of ten to forty times what can be naturally replenished. In one significant Iowa rainstorm in 2013, five inches was lost in one day. All the more alarming is that this loss occurred in a place that in the mid-1800s had topsoil depths of fourteen inches that are now around six inches, and where such facts equal a forty-dollar-per-acre annual financial hit for farmers, or billions each year. That washed-away topsoil produces silted riverways and a biologically dead Gulf of Mexico.

Practices like no-till farming increase soil life, fertility, and moisture retention—reducing the need for inputs that also hurt a farmer's bottom line. And there are programs like Iowa State University's Science-based Trials of Rowcrops Integrated with Prairie Strips (STRIPS) that are working to curb soil loss and nutrient runoff by up to 90 percent. By strategically planting thin strips of prairie grasses and forbs—commonly along low areas or slopes—most soil and nutrients can be kept in place, filtered, and recovered. Preserving rich soil matters when you consider that in the next twenty to fifty years we will produce 30 percent less food as soil degrades and as need rises 50 percent. Part of the answer will likely be mimicking the prairie in our agricultural systems. Soil microbes recycle organic matter and engineer the soil, making it more resilient and able to hold more water. A team of scientists at UC Boulder have begun analyzing subsoil microbial communities present in virgin prairie, taking samples mostly from old country cemeteries up and down the eastern Plains. Bacteria in the phylum Verrucomicrobia were found in great quantities; they are not found in highly fertilized, tilled fields. These bacteria thrive in poor-nutrient soils and may help break down carbohydrates to enrich soil minerals, but much is still unknown about their role in historic prairie communities.

A group of researchers from the University of Nebraska has begun examining a portion of a centuries-old sod house from Custer County in western Nebraska, a place with more sod buildings than anywhere else in North America. The three-room house was built in 1902 and 1903 by Henry Eugene Chrisman, and the walls should reveal insects and grassland plant species present at the time, as well as possible non-native and invasive plant species. In addition, the soil will be able to show how much fertility has been lost over 110 years and what effect this loss may have on future remnants and restorations.

Why are we looking at soil, microbes, and prairie? Because we are realizing how little we know about our world or how it works—and that we often leap before looking, assuming we know best and discounting the vast and complicated knowledge of other species, let alone entire ecosystems. Native plants create communities that thrive above and below the soil line. Their roots harbor beneficial microbes just as those roots amend soil. A well-positioned, healthy stand of native prairie, even among a field of corn, can fundamentally alter nearby ecology and mitigate human-caused negative impacts on the landscape. What could a similar stand do in housing divisions or other urban areas? But it's not just native plants that have special relationships with soil life, it's also invasive exotics.

Marnie Rout of the University of North Texas Health Science Center drove by a prairie remnant one day and noticed how a line was drawn down the middle—to one side was prairie, to the other invasive sorghum. She and her colleagues looked into the soils beneath the sorghum and found higher levels of nitrogen and phosphorous, and then wondered what could account for this within the soil life. They found bacterial strains of endophytes, found inside sorghum rhizomes, that helped fix nitrogen, phosphorous, and iron in the soil; the last mineral can be toxic to many crops, and in large enough quantities may even inhibit prairie species. As we learn about our soil, we learn about our plant communities, as well as the fauna they support. It's an amazing, mind-blowing, and exciting biological system with untapped potential for home landscapes.

Couldn't prairies exist in our backyards in some meaningful form? The original idea behind suburbs was one vast expanse of parkland, lawn being the great equalizer and democratizer where everyone had a similar stake. Instead of lawn, why couldn't we have some form of prairie? Why couldn't roadsides be some sort of grassland? Why couldn't medians and hellstrips, portions of parks and playing fields, church and school landscapes? What are the lessons we can learn from wilder areas to help us better create and manage semi-wildness in urban centers? What happens to our world when we start learning from its complexity instead of teaching it how to be simple and one-dimensional? We supposedly prize diversity and health among our own species, but more openly despise it among others and the ecosystems they need to thrive. We proclaim ourselves right in a wrong world, instead of, potentially, wrong in a right world.

I don't see much that is humble or inquisitive in gardens composed of hosta, daylily, barberry, miscanthus, Russian sage, or feather reed grass—plants that have no shared evolutionary history with wildlife in any area of North America. I don't see much in the way of compassion, respect, community, mercy, or love in gardens composed of plants like this, because these gardens are not reaching out to the essential wildness still among us; such gardens are not seeking to bridge the divide, but only to keep it wide. I don't see much in the way of wanting to learn about local ecological processes or living history of place, though we celebrate and foster other aspects of our local culture and daily lives, from sports to festivals to volunteerism. I don't see much of wanting to help wildlife adapt to the world we're taking away from them through industrial agriculture, lawns, concrete, and an altered climate.

The argument for fair play and hybrid benefits is commonly made for mixing native plants and regionally adapted plants, the latter a synonym for non-native plants that thrive in local conditions and so far have not been invasive. Often, the line of reasoning is that we don't have to sacrifice ecology for beauty from around the world, and that we should be free to use whatever we want in our landscapes that is pretty, brings us joy, and is low maintenance. In other words, we conflate our culture with plant culture so we can justify our actions.

But plant culture is not human culture. Our definition of freedom and equality and the pursuit of happiness have little to do with nature or ecosystem function. Planting a mix of natives and exotics, for example, is not the same as having equal access to education, marriage, or voting. It is a dangerous supposition when we translate human culture—all of our good and all of our ills—onto plant culture, or onto nature in general. In some ways, doing so is an act of appropriation and destruction, forcing ourselves and our perspectives onto other living organisms and entire living systems.

To respect life, you have to respect the place it comes from—the culture of its existence—and let it develop its culture of place. We barely understand a prairie's culture, a complex structure formed over countless generations where mutualism and exclusion create healthy and resilient ecosystems above and below the soil line. In many human cultures, a prairie culture—the prairie ecosystem itself—would seem destructive and undemocratic. A prairie would be harsh, unrealistic, unfair, and totalitarian, and maybe that's why we've eradicated so much of it in America.

Democracy is not giving all plants a fair shot in the garden. Democracy is respecting the revived ecosystem, the place of native plants and wild relationships, their shared history and mutualism, their reliance upon one another through evolutionary trial and error. When we step in and impose our ideals of democracy on a landscape, we disrupt and destroy the landscape, altering life processes that have worked long before we created human democracy; life processes that thrive, in many ways, on principles that oppose democracy. And yet, respecting an ecosystem enough not to erode or incorrectly micromanage it also exercises human concepts of democracy—the pursuit of happiness, life, and liberty, the ability to practice any religion you want to or believe in any philosophy or live according to your gender identity.

Gardens by default are already problematic. When we move plants or alter their arrangement, we destroy or remake their culture. We take away their inalienable rights and remove from the equation some degree of what they can teach us about intercultural relations and understanding. This reality is something we can't fully escape. However, when we plow up a prairie, we erase an opportunity to improve our existence, to develop compassion, and to avoid thinking of ourselves as better than someone else. How we use wild plants from wild areas like prairies in urban gardens says as much about plant culture as it does our culture. Unfortunately, our species has a long history of distrust, alienation, and genocide—the last of which is an act of erasure, whether through fear or misunderstanding, but always from a root of thinking one group superior to another, and the needs of one as being the needs of the many. Too often, built landscapes (and more and more what's left of nature) are a reflection of our superiority. Even if gardens are art—our way to bridge the gap between us and nature through a cultural interpretation of beauty—there will always be an element of extreme privilege; the question is how much privilege and what it says about our core beliefs.

Native plant gardens are not looking backward, trying to recreate an environment that can no longer exist in a place like a highway median or urban park or backyard oasis. My city will never be the prairie it was a hundred and fifty years ago, and if humans vanished tomorrow, it would not become, in another hundred and fifty years, the prairie it once was. The loss of that prairie is an indictment and a travesty, and yet we are still surrounded by its wildness—and the lives that make up the remnants and travel the thin corridors between them. Using native plants is not about going back in time; it is, however, about going forward and helping flora and fauna adapt to a world we're altering at breakneck speed. But they still exist, those flora and fauna, and to garden simply for ourselves is not an appropriate answer to mass extinction or climate change or polluted waterways or heat islands or dirty air.

Maybe it ultimately comes down to this: native plants are some-times seen as a threat, whether that's a conscious or subconscious response. Native plants are a threat to an entire Western culture, and an entire industry, built foremost on nature as ornamentation for human visual consumption. Native plants represent a garden-ing paradigm that, instead of focusing solely or primarily on the commercialization of our five senses, explores the deeper issues of why we garden, how we garden, and who we garden for. We are asked to stop and think critically in unfamiliar and uncomfortable ways that challenge and test our assumptions as well as our per-sonal identities. These issues are nothing new; instead, they are poking holes in generations of embedded acceptance that nature is for us, and that how we rearrange it is by default noble, good, and environmentally benign. Or, since we are a part of nature, how we influence it is, to some degree, part of a natural process—especially if it's to give people joy through a sublime vista that's pleasing to the eye.

Every year new hybrids of plants come out, as do new "discov-eries" made halfway across the world. These plants are pushed and promoted as products to consume, like new phones, which feels disrespectful to the natural communities we hope to positively im-pact. Not only do so many "new" plants come to us relatively un-proven in home and urban landscapes, they may not even support the wildlife community we assume they'll benefit. Excitement for plants and gardening is wonderful—we need more of it—and yet the gateway drug cannot be solely beauty for our own consumption; it needs to be, and many are calling for it to be, what the plant is doing beyond its aesthetic appearance. That we find plants pretty is both dumb luck and, one might suspect, a product of our shared ancestry, chemicals, interdependency, biophilia, et cetera. If we can't recognize or discuss the deeper beauty of plants, then judging them by their attractiveness is as shallow and culturally indicting as valuing a person on their appearance or the kind of car they drive.

While native plants may sometimes be seen as a threat to culture and industry, they also offer an immense opportunity. We've created a human-centered system based on visual appeal and commerce, but we can go beyond greenwashing plant tags or calling hybrids native plants. We can say native plants aren't just for us, that in fact they are for everything but us, and in that act revolutionize why we garden, how we garden, and who we garden for. We'll create a new level of impactful community action. Suddenly, something radical happens as we stop thinking about gardens as primarily for us, or at least view them as a fifty/fifty proposition. This selflessness begins to spread into other areas of our lives. Those practicing permaculture know this, as do the countless vendors in local farmer's markets. Social justice begins, in part, with environmental justice—and maybe even with wildlife justice. Equality for other species will augment and spur equality among our own species.

Don't let anyone say natives are "limiting," or that advocating for them is "finger wagging" or "puritanical preaching." The truth is, using native plants awakens us to our negative (and positive) role on this planet, something we don't want to address or confess; that's human nature. The deeper conversation is not about native plants, even though we seldom realize it or address it. Instead, the conversation is about a burgeoning awareness of how we have forever altered the world, often in destructive and terrifyingly unpredictable ways, and that to change our course means changes to our safe, comfortable assumptions that are culturally and corporately defined.

Native plant gardening does not limit your aesthetic choices; it expands your ethical ones, connecting you to your family, your children, your children's children, and all other humans and species who are bound together in ways we ignore in every aspect of our privileged Western lives. We are a navel-gazing group, and at the first call to think beyond the self, we expend more energy denying real freedom than enacting it. That's freedom to have clean air, safe water, a sound agricultural system full of beneficial pollinators, and a secure economy based on all of the above. Native plants in a garden may not save the environment, but they'll certainly get us thinking about when and why the environment needs saving, and how to think in a radical new way to make it happen.

When we embrace the conversation's subsequent feelings of anger, denial, grief, and loss, we become something much better. We become agents of super-positive change—stronger, more resilient, and beacons of faith in action. Our landscapes become selfless acts of defiance. Our gardens become homecomings for countless species, including ourselves. Native plants are limiting? Only if you garden just for yourself.

This fall, after the first full year of my back-lawn-to-meadow conversion, I twice walked through a banded spider's web. She had created a small triangle between a two-foot-tall sunflower and an eight-inch-tall blade of sideoats grama. The first time I stepped into her weave, I was weeding foxtail, and only noticed what I'd done because of the tug against my bare legs—spider silk is stronger than the Kevlar in bulletproof vests. The second time I walked through her web, I was just careless. But each time I stopped to apologize. Maybe this act could be dismissed as bluestem-hugging nonsense, something a silly child might do, but then again maybe we need more hippy children. Maybe the spider was understanding or angry, maybe she was communicating in ways I couldn't perceive. Maybe we need more communication of any kind even if we can't or have forgotten how to speak the language of the world around us—of spiders and sunflowers and sideoats grama.

One way to learn that language again is to explore the remnants of wildness around us, in prairies and woodlands and deserts and fens. Another way is to bring that wildness home—and to see how much more wildness is waiting at the margins of our lives to flow into the very heart of our daily being. The number of spiders, beetles, butterflies, bees, and more seems to double every time I expand the gardens at home. My lawn, a default mode of landscape that required weekly mowing, now requires one or two days of intense annual management. My lawn, something that helped me blend in with my neighbors, has been replaced with thousands and thousands of native plants that help me connect with the prairie remnant just one mile south of me, the other remnant six miles north, and the larger world beyond. We are nature; all of our hopes and passions for a better world rest in the blooms and roots and are cast out on the backs of birds and insects reaching for the horizon.

CHAPTER 3

Why We Believe
What We Believe

Once you see it, you can't unsee it.
And once you've seen it, keeping quiet,
saying nothing, becomes as political an act
as speaking out. There's no innocence.
Either way, you're accountable.

— Arundhati Roy

V IEWING A GARDEN from a distance is akin to holding a
book without reading the words. At best, the perception is
a smearing of color, a global sense of forms and textures, or the
essence of a faint smell and the hint of movement between the
blooms. Gardens should be experienced so close you risk getting
stung or bitten, or contracting an itch that no cream will sooth.
You have to brave your senses and sense of reality.

We have to risk our arms and noses, because this is where life
meets us in the garden—those intimate moments we long for in
any type of nature. I didn't used to smell milkweed blooms, as
there didn't seem to be much point; they weren't fragrant from
ten feet or ten inches away, at least not the species I grew. Common milkweed, on the other hand, in its peak summer bloom out
in a field or meadow—that's something you can smell from ten
feet away, a spicy-sweet, creamy vanilla. I had just one fledgling

common milkweed bloom in the back of the garden, and you had to work through the bramble to get to it.

Milkweed flowers are incredibly complex, not to mention sinister. To be pollinated, an insect must place its legs deep down into a narrow notch, and then do so again on another bloom on another plant; it's like playing Plinko on *The Price Is Right* and hoping to hit big money. The sinister part is that the narrow notch is so tight and so sticky that many insects lose their legs trying to leave, while others end up unable to free themselves and die of starvation and exposure.

One day when I saw a honey bee nestled in a flower, I thought little of it—it was stuck or maybe just resting. I didn't even see the camouflaged crab spider secured to the bee until I sat down in the shade to look over the images I'd taken on the camera. But there it was, nature red in tooth and claw. I have seldom felt so fulfilled, knowing that this garden isn't necessarily here to make me feel good about myself or bring me pleasure or solace. No, the garden is here to promote death as much as life. From the predators to the winter stems left standing where bee larvae slumber, the garden is what we can't see from a distance—even what we'll never see or completely understand. Gardens make us wonderfully vulnerable to the language and the culture of others.

We live in a world of wounds. Not only the wounds we face in our daily lives—the struggles of poverty, violence, loss, and even love—but the wounds of our diverse cultures and societies that demand we live up to certain realities and expectations. We might be expected to live on our own at a certain age, marry a specific kind of person, or hold ourselves back if we disagree with another's point of view. Then we have wounds born from our genes, that are a part of our evolution as a wild species trying to survive the real and perceived physical dangers of finding food and shelter or escaping predators and disease. It's hard enough being human, being animal, and then on top of it all, we create complex social systems, often with the addition of conflicting layers of ethics and morality that influence our beliefs and actions. Our education might tell us that the Arctic will soon be ice free, which will warm the world faster, or that everyone has the same fundamental rights, but the culture we're raised in at home or work might profess the exact opposite.

Now let's add the wounds of the real world—those places and species beyond our human walls that make up 99.9 percent of all life. Consider turtles taken from their wild homes for the pet trade or Karner blue butterflies with no wild lupine to lay eggs on or rusty patched bumble bees with no tallgrass prairie. And when you account for not just how we treat ourselves—our racism, sexism, and classism—but also how we treat other species or our local landscapes, and the weight of some moral or ethical code that extends beyond ourselves to "lesser" species may seem far too complicated and unbearable. Those codes may feel like too much of a leap for our simple minds, evolutionarily hardwired to avoid obvious physical threats in the immediate sphere, and not the sprawling, amorphous blobs of thoughtful, far-thinking, far-hearted action. Humans are animals, driven by instinct and yet motivated by something beyond instinct. How can we learn to see threats to others as threats to ourselves, and so take appropriate action?

Consider this line of reasoning from activist and author Barry Lopez, borrowed from his book *Arctic Dreams*:

> Because mankind can circumvent evolutionary law, it is incumbent upon him, say evolutionary biologists, to develop another law to abide by if he wishes to survive, to not outstrip his food base. He must learn restraint. He must derive some other, wiser way of behaving toward the land. He must be more attentive to the biological imperatives of the system of sun-driven protoplasm upon which he, too, is still dependent. Not because he must, because he lacks inventiveness, but because herein is the accomplishment of the wisdom that for centuries he has aspired to. Having taken on his own destiny, he must now think with

critical intelligence about where to defer.... No culture has
yet solved the dilemma each has faced with the growth of
a conscious mind: how to live a moral and compassionate
existence when one is fully aware of the blood, the horror
inherent in all life, when one finds darkness not only in one's
own culture but within oneself.

How profound to think that our wisdom is evolutionary—that
our idea of right and wrong has been encoded and grown in us
over eons, perhaps in response to our ability to be both stewards
and destroyers. Our capacity for compassion is infinite, deep, and
richly complex, and it probably needs to be, to ensure not just our
very real, everyday survival in a wild world, but also the everyday survival of that real world—and the millions of species whose
rights to exist are as necessary as our own. Perhaps the ultimate
empathy is to not move a rock, not cast the milkweed fluff, not
drive into that field, not step in the path of a beetle. Perhaps action
begins with the subtlest inaction. Respect is not just being polite;
respect is compassion borne out from knowing our existence is
shared equally and that we are not infallibly right.

The above thoughts make discussing issues such as climate
change and extinction slippery. It is a conversation that has been
usurped by politics, turning it into a polarized and divisive subject based lopsidedly on opinion and emotion, and playing on our
worst fears, which are grounded in our personal backgrounds.
It's the same thing that happens when we talk about gardens and
native plants. We become polarized as we defend our preconceptions, our business and our art, our culture and our social sphere.
Maybe in exploring climate change and the psychology around
it, we can learn how to more effectively discuss landscapes and
how our gardens can be rethought to work in the context of a new
world.

You've heard this before: almost every scientist who studies
Earth systems agrees we are in the sixth mass extinction brought
on by significant, forever-altering climate change induced by

human use of fossil fuels and habitat destruction. Our first response to this fact might be sadness. We may say something like, "That makes me sad," and then move on from the subject. That response rings slightly hollow, though, because it comes from a place of defense. We feel that we must guard against fully embracing and comprehending what climate change or extinction is, lest we risk losing our minds and our neatly packaged sense of social stability. When we say the reality of extinction makes us sad, we may also be saying there's too much reality in that thought. We can say the event is sad and acknowledge the reality while simultaneously brushing it aside.

I don't want us to waste time being sad because it's not often a deep feeling that engenders change or empowering action. Sadness is an easy place to rest in doubt and confusion as it's strangely comforting and safe. No, I want us angry, mad, pissed off. I want sadness to quickly feed defiant compassion, to carry us into real, actionable solutions that radically and fundamentally change how and why we live on this planet. Let's harness sadness to help us learn. I want us to hold the butterfly in our hands, emerging too early to find nectar. I want us to see the nest of young mourning doves left precariously alone all day because the parents are out frantically looking for insects. I want us to say one afternoon, "Huh, there seem to be fewer bees this year," and to find the research that supports this observation. Every action we take carries weight and importance and liberating power, for us and for other species. What we do or don't do defines who we are, and it's the same for what we believe and don't believe. What will we do when we learn about our role in altering the world? How will our gardens evolve as our ethics evolve? How will we steward entire regions as our local garden stewardship shifts perspectives?

A 2013 report from the Intergovernmental Panel on Climate Change summarized a six-year study entitled "Climate Change 2013: The Physical Science Basis." Six hundred scientists from 39 countries assessed nine thousand peer-reviewed studies culminating in countless graphs, tables, and research that show the increase in surface temperatures has already surpassed 2° Celsius in many parts of the world, a limit that we are not supposed to surpass if we hope to preserve Earth's functioning climatic systems like ocean currents that regulate global temperatures. Rising temperatures from heat-trapping carbon and methane have led us to the sixth mass extinction. The fifth extinction 66 million years ago released one to two gigatonnes of CO_2 that radically changed the global environment, leading to the erasure of 76 percent of all species. We currently release 30 gigatonnes of CO_2 each year, while methane and other even more destructive elements continue to increase and speed up planetary disruption. In fact, as the soil warms, its life forms grow and reproduce. Instead of soil acting as a carbon sink, in the way that grasslands operate, the soil life will be releasing far more atmospheric carbon than soils or plants can absorb. By 2050 once colder regions that hold frozen permafrost could release 55 trillion kilograms of carbon, equal to the predicted amount of carbon emissions for the United States during that same time period.

Tracking changes species by species in these or even normal conditions is difficult. We simply can't know or monitor every life form on the planet, let alone fully understand their interactions with their environments and other species. This reality does not give us a pass, though. It would be a logical fallacy to think that, since we don't know all that is happening, maybe we're not losing anything significant and things will ultimately turn out okay. The collective knowledge of the world's organisms and environments far outstrips our own, and when we lose that knowledge, we lose the ability to better comprehend or care for the world. If we look at the International Union for Conservation of Nature's Red List, those species most at threat from vanishing in the near future, we see a total number of 83,000. A recent analysis explored 8,700 of those species that are near-threatened or threatened and represent larger groups where all known species have been fully assessed. The analysis showed that the three main drivers of biodiversity loss are the same for all threatened species: overexploitation (mostly harvesting of species), agriculture (production of food, fodder, fibers, and fuel crops, as well as livestock, aquaculture, and tree cultivation), and urban development.

Of those species reviewed, more than 6,200 are at risk from overexploitation, 5,400 from agriculture, and 3,000 from urban development. Of all plant, amphibian, reptile, bird, and mammal species that have gone extinct since the year 1500, 75 percent were significantly harmed by overexploitation, agriculture, or both. It is obvious that we either don't know or don't care how to work with the life on this planet—to cohabit for mutual health and survival. Part of this reality surely stems from a consumer-driven, capitalist-based global market, one that equates freedom with the ability to buy and sell. But part of it might also stem from our inability to ethically respond to and emotionally evolve with the world we're transforming so quickly.

The loss of overall biodiversity, based on the number of genetically unique ecological niches, is our largest threat to a livable world, for the very reason that it provides redundancies or safeguards for the health and evolution of our planet. We don't know what small, out-of-the-way creature may already be or may become an important part of some larger plan. Take, for example, the meltwater stonefly in Glacier National Park, a place that since 1850 has seen 85 percent of its glaciers erased and will be completely ice-free by 2020. The fly lives in a very specific niche: the freezing cold water coming off glaciers. Over the summer, stoneflies move upstream to find the coldest conditions, and as they do so, mini populations become separated from one another. A group or even an individual that might be adapting to warmer conditions downstream can't interact, or share its genes, with the larger groups moving upstream. Will the loss of this seemingly innocuous species be more telling down the road, or will we let it be telling right now? What are we risking when we lose even the smallest species?

Changes in ecosystems due to rising temperatures also affect other organisms like cottonwood trees, specifically individual genotypes; distinct cottonwoods can support seven hundred insect species as well as other life forms such as beavers, bacteria, lichen, and soil microbes, so the loss of a genetically unique population of cottonwood trees could have an unpredictable cascade effect. And this is just one tree. What other effects will be felt due to the loss of ice and a warming of the climate? What species or ecosystems will exist one day and be gone the next simply because we're heating our homes and driving to the big-box store and buying new clothes?

Overall, species that have the lowest level of genetic diversity will get hit the hardest by climate change, unable to adapt or evolve over any period of time. The places where such genetically invariable species live generally have fewer organisms because the conditions there are already so harsh—like the cold, icy streams that the meltwater stonefly calls home. Those species are called "restricted endemics" and tend to live in one of 35 global biodiversity hotspots, places with 1,500 or more native species but only 30 percent or less of habitat remaining.

Loss of habitat can be partially overcome if species are able to move and share their genetic material. Diverse and linked ecosystems that allow migration are crucial, acting as a climate change buffer by helping as many species as possible adapt, even if their numbers are relatively low. These ecosystems may better withstand climatic swings while providing all sorts of ecosystem services like mitigating floods, sequestering carbon, and reducing disease. An analysis published in *Science* authored by scientists from 14 countries found that dryland ecosystems are the most threatened. They cover 40 percent of the Earth's surface and support 40 percent of the human population, but are particularly vulnerable to environmental changes and desertification.

Another report that appeared in *Nature* goes even further. The findings show that, within two years after a significant climate event that disturbed the environment (floods, drought, et cetera), low-diversity communities with just one or two plant species experienced a productivity loss of 50 percent, while high-diversity communities of 16 to 32 species changed only by 25 percent. The conclusions are that biodiversity stabilizes an ecosystem and lessens swings in ecosystem services. In an uncertain future, it would seem maintaining biologic diversity that works together in a tight-knit system is paramount, and that coevolved biodiversity would be the most resilient.

With unpredictable and more intense climatic swings induced by higher concentrations of greenhouse gases, biodiversity can do more than buffer the loss of wildlife or the threats of extreme weather events. When the USSR collapsed, communal farming systems collapsed with it. This led to farmers heading for cities to find work, abandoning 110 million acres of farmland that then went wild. What at first glance appears to be large-scale human failure actually turns out to be an environmental success, as the vegetation now growing on those fields absorbs 50 million tons of carbon each year, or roughly 10 percent of Russia's annual carbon emissions.

Soil is an amazing carbon sink, and we are learning how to increase carbon storage in traditional agriculture through methods such as crop rotation and buffer strips of prairie. Yet new research points to the fact that our soils might not be as good at storing carbon as we once hoped. Data from Northern Arizona University shows that while increased levels of atmospheric CO_2 will promote more photosynthesis and plant growth, thereby increasing the potential to absorb CO_2, increased soil carbon may also spur microbes to produce CO_2 as they break down that carbon. The estimates are that higher levels of CO_2 in the air will increase plant-based carbon sequestration by 20 percent, but that soil microbes will put back 16.5 percent of that CO_2 into the air. Uncertainty, though, is our new future. How can we be certain how the world will respond to our increasing pressures upon it? How can we be certain what oceans, soils, and plants will do? We're not even certain what's being lost—though as with climate change, we do have a pretty good idea.

Plants and animals disappear all the time. Evolution works in this way, and we are likely to have never had the good fortune of knowing many of those extinct species. Maybe they were naturally outcompeted, succumbed to a disease, or evolved into a new form. But the background extinction rate, that level at which species are naturally erased, is far lower than currently observed rates. One international study, led by Gerardo Ceballos of the Instituto de Ecologia in Mexico, used as a baseline rate two mammal extinctions per 10,000 species per 100 years, a rate twice as high as is commonly used. The authors then compared this rate to conservative estimates of the current rate of vertebrate losses over the last century, finding those losses to be 100 times greater than the background rate. Previous estimates suggest that number of species should have taken anywhere from eight hundred to ten thousand years to vanish. Just in the islands of Oceania, up to 1,800 bird species have been extirpated since human contact some two thousand years ago. In the end, for every degree of global temperature rise, we can expect a 3 percent rise in species extinction, and may face a 16 percent species loss or more by the end of the century.

What these many studies add up to is this: the world has lost one-tenth of its wilderness in just the last 20 years. That's an area the size of Alaska. There's still 11.6 million square miles of relatively intact wilderness left in the world, mainly in northern Asia, northern Canada, and north Africa—all places fairly inhospitable to humans to this point. But there's wildness in other places, too. Aquatic life may be the most threatened of all as more carbon is absorbed by oceans, acidifying them and lowering oxygen levels. Acidification is currently accelerating faster than it has in the last 300 million years, or the period that marked the Permian extinction when 95 percent of ocean life was lost; then, it took 30 million years for the oceans to recover. Remember that rate of CO_2 release into the atmosphere of 30 gigatonnes per year? That's a rate 10 times faster than 300 million years ago. Sure, life will recover, new species will emerge and evolve—but how many of us will be around in tens of millions of years to enjoy the falsely comforting prediction that "life finds a way"?

The entire world is now a garden—a space altered by human influence—and this understanding creates some stark realities in how we rethink the most intimate places we inhabit and are exposed to every day: our suburban lots, our urban roadways, our parks and schoolyards. While we are causing biodiversity loss in mammals, arthropods, and more, it's incumbent upon us to follow the food chain and understand how natural systems work, what life up and down the trophic level needs to thrive and adapt, and what we can do about it. That's where exploring the issues surrounding plants come in.

The news on plants isn't rosy, but if organisms that use plants are in trouble, then it makes sense that the further down the chain you go, the more precarious the situation becomes. We know of roughly 390,000 plant species, with around 2,000 being discovered every year. As with animals and insects, we aren't likely to fully know their functions or how they interact with their environments. It takes a lot of time and money to quantify ecological function for any one organism. The UK's Kew Royal Botanic Gardens recently revealed in its State of the World's Plants that at least one-fifth of global plant species are at risk of extinction due to a perfect storm of habitat loss, disease, and invasive species—all exacerbated by climate change. This threat of extinction is one reason why biologist E.O. Wilson proposes his "Half-Earth" idea— the goal of setting aside 50 percent of the most biodiverse areas on Earth and essentially leaving them free to their own devices to adapt and evolve.

In his book *Plant Conservation: Why It Matters and How It Works*, Timothy Walker makes several startling claims, one of which is that by 2050 we may have lost almost 30 percent of all global plant species. Such loss begs the question: which of these plant species could have cured cancer, or Alzheimer's, or given us the clues to cleaner energy? One hundred years from now, only 8 percent of current protected lands—refuges and the like—will be in the right place to conserve species who use them, as climate change forces species uphill and to the north to find their coevolved niches. Some 276 of our national parks are experiencing springs weeks ahead of schedule, which might require us to expand or move their boundaries to protect wildlife.

Built landscapes play a complicated if not deleterious role in the environment. According to Walker, private and botanic gardens are in fact the number one threat to biodiversity due to the potential release of invasive plants: this claim, though radical, is essential. How do we know if or when a plant from another region will become invasive? How do we know what the interactions will be above and below the soil line? Or how such a plant will become a part of its larger environment, for good or ill? If we know so very little about the life on our world, how can we presume that our garden plant choices are right just because we think they are pretty, make us happy, or foster some sense of human freedom? We desperately need to more critically question our choices and beliefs. In fact, we need to go even further and directly challenge our beliefs in order to test our assumptions about them.

Plants escape gardens and alter environments from the soil on up. Invasive plants contribute to even greater biodiversity loss and complete ecosystem alterations that might take millions of years to rebalance. Our current, relatively easy lifestyle has been given to us by several layers of biotic redundancy—meaning, the planet can take a licking and keep on ticking…to a point. And we may be at that point where the Goldilocks era of our planet is over: a perfectly balanced moment in time that has seen the greatest number of species working in highly functional equilibrium. It's that equilibrium which has helped our diverse human cultures develop and flourish.

With the above information in mind, it's clear that a changing climate, caused by humans, is going to have deep and powerful repercussions on biodiversity, adaptability, and health. We don't know what we're doing, and even if we did know down to the letter, would that spur necessary change? If we knew, without a shadow of a doubt, that specific native plants in our region were performing a plethora of specific ecosystem services, would we be more careful to use those plants in place of others? If we all knew how important our garden landscapes were to wildlife, soil remediation, water and air purification, and our own health, would we demand far more from our designers and contractors? Would we become a more integrated and humble part of the way the world functions? Would we reshape our economy and government as a result?

Statistics may sway those of us who think analytically and prize scientific inquiry, but not necessarily those who go more by emotions and instinct, by in-the-gut daily interactions with life around them. And when that life, that wildness, is absent or diminished, what emotional connection can we have beyond those we have with our children, our domesticated pets, and a few resilient or opportunistic birds, rodents, and butterflies? Sometimes statistics and research are just a way to discuss a subject by avoiding it. We know what's wrong, what's at stake, even without every last shred of analysis. Those statistics may simply be a way to carefully delay the emotional pain and trauma that will predicate our necessary outward changes. We certainly know that native plants, in their wild environments and in the cultivated wild of the urban and suburban, are critical components to our wellbeing. Maybe we don't put enough faith in the wisdom and order of systems that are more in sync and balance than we've become. We don't have to use native plants—we make a choice when we do or don't use them—but in that decision resonates our depth of empathy and compassion, as well as our own ability to adapt and evolve.

From about July 1 to September 1 of each year, I often have to enjoy the garden from behind glass. My three daily walks are relegated to one evening sprint after the Sun's heat has subsided, even as the humidity remains ridiculously high. And then there are the mosquitoes who find my garden a nirvana. After dinner I may slide open the door and briskly step into the soup, then slice through the overgrown plants crowding the narrow paths, all in a scant five minutes, barely enough time to notice daily changes. So I stand inside by the cool air vent hoping to see something new playing out in the landscape—but it will have to be obvious, like birds chasing one another or a dead tree limb falling to the ground. Or butterflies coasting in on a southerly breeze. I don't usually see a good deal of butterflies or moths until mid- to late summer, when their generations have finally built up in large enough numbers to saturate the environment. I especially don't tend to see monarchs until around my birthday in mid-July, so on one early afternoon as the backyard sizzles, I see a dash of orange on a *Liatris* that pulls me outside with my three cameras in tow.

The butterfly is thirty feet from the house, and as I get nearer, I realize it's not acting like a monarch. Monarchs are very flighty. They're especially cautious, seeing each bloom as a safe haven and everything else as dangerous lava, like the game I played as a child jumping on living room furniture. This butterfly was far more patient and methodical, taking its time, not even excited into the air when a stiff breeze came up. I soon realized it was a queen butterfly, rare this far north. The image I took found its way to an entomologist who said it was from a Texas population. After that first summer, I've seen a queen every subsequent summer, three or four years in a row now, usually the first week in August. Its appearance is like clockwork.

I didn't notice the gargantuan praying mantis on a *Liatris* stalk six inches away from the queen until I downloaded the pictures to my computer. But there it was, a Chinese mantis, a species quickly overspreading native species like the Carolina mantis, which is much smaller. Those Chinese mantises are so big and powerful they can wrangle cicadas and hummingbirds, so a queen or swallowtail butterfly is no problem. In fact, over the years, I've encountered dozens of sets of monarch wings littering the ground beneath all sorts of blooms, castoffs from a mantis meal. Those wings are now scattered on bookshelves in my office, and when I walk by they easily take flight, as if they were still part of a living body.

But I haven't always seen these things in the garden—monarch wings, the Chinese mantis, or queen butterflies. I'm not going to chalk it up to climate change alone, or the success of my lush garden. I know something is happening. I feel this subtle tear in the world, and I want to know why it is, and what it means. I wonder if I'm doing something wrong.

We exist in a world of wounds, and yet we don't, can't, or won't recognize those wounds. Doing so is an essential step in bridging scientific fact with emotion, a step that can lead to empowered action. With a world in a biodiversity crisis, author Robert Macfarlane says, "we register that crisis…as an ambient hum of guilt, easily faded out.like other unwholesome aspects of the Anthropocene, we mostly respond to mass extinction with stuplimity: the aesthetic experience in which astonishment is united with boredom, such that we overload on anxiety to the point of outrage-outage. Art and literature might, at their best, shock us out of the stuplime."[1] I wonder how gardens and large urban landscapes might work as pieces of ecological art to shock us out of the stuplime. But I also wonder how our current urban landscapes foster a vicious cycle of the stuplime, or more accurately, unethical amnesia. How might they do this? Maybe by privileging one species over another through vast stretches of lawn, ill-timed mowing, monocultures of exotic plants that share no evolutionary history with wildlife. Do our landscapes exhibit a sense of boredom? Do we at least innately know that this boredom results not only in diminishing ourselves, but in diminishing nature as well?

Maybe these sterilized landscapes also awaken a lingering sense that our individual choices, guaranteed to us by declarations of freedom in the constitution, are not as benign as we're led to believe. I can think of no greater act of patriotism than ensuring the health of a biodiverse land base, whether it's in wildlife refuges, agricultural fields, or front yards. But we're not acting very patriotically. We're not exactly ethical creatures in the truest democratic sense. We conveniently forget what that sense is when it confronts our beliefs about ourselves, as well as our lifestyle. Sometimes we even reframe or reposition our ethics to defend ourselves, all the while aware of how precarious that makes our argument.

When we act unethically, we tend to remember those actions less clearly, a phenomenon based in the fact that we feel uncomfortable remembering ourselves acting in ways we shouldn't. Behavioral research specialist Maryam Kouchaki from the Kellogg School of Management at Northwestern University and Francesca Gino from the Harvard Business School studied 2,100 individuals as they uncovered the concept of unethical amnesia. They say "[it] is driven by the desire to lower one's distress that comes from acting unethically and to maintain a positive self image as a moral individual." In general, people limit the retrieval of memories that threaten their moral self-concept, and that's why unethical behaviors may be so pervasive across individuals and groups.

If this deliberate forgetfulness is true, then are we all constant hypocrites, subconsciously denying ourselves true efficacy and resisting the evolution of our species? Do any of us walk the walk in a pure enough way in our relationship with nature so as to never be hypocritical? Probably not, and if we did, perhaps our sense of personal and cultural right or wrong would be less clear, and our emotions less directive. What I mean is, when I snuck up behind grasshoppers to capture and feed them to a yellow garden spider, I didn't feel bad at first. My inquisitiveness was justified by my sense of superiority over the landscape. Early in my gardening life during a particularly bad year, I liberally applied diatomaceous earth to the garden, a silica mineral which is supposed to get under the grasshopper's exoskeleton and rip open their insides, killing them. Of course, this product can also harm far more life in the garden, but I didn't know that. My eagerness to solve a temporary problem far outweighed any constructive, ethical thinking. My plants, my vision for them, was more important than the natural grasshopper and locust cycles of the region I lived in and knew little about. In the end, my choices had far more brutal consequences than letting nature take its course. The silica, in effect, tore open my own insides.

Perhaps this thinking is radical and unrelatable. Maybe it makes me crazy, seeing other lives and the world beyond myself as equal to or more important than myself. Especially if this understanding leads me to challenge the views of others. I wonder how we experience ethical amnesia in regards to climate change, or using non-native plants in our gardens.

As an environmental activist, the first words that get hurled at me are "tree hugger" and "vegan," neither of which I am—and even if I were, what's wrong with that? I don't hug trees, I burn them, especially red cedars in order to open up land for prairie. If anything, I hug bluestem and milkweed. But once again we create labels to remove us from discomfort or knowing things that will make us call into question our lifestyles, or beliefs, or our culture in general. How do we recognize, cope with, and use these complex feelings to evolve as stewards of life and not just dominators or manipulators of life?

If we look at the issues surrounding extinction and climate change, it's not that people don't care per se, it's that our emotional response to these issues creates incredible anxiety and despair. We feel powerless as individuals and groups. In a piece on climate change psychology for the *Huffington Post*, Renee Lertzman notes that information on the largest challenge our species has ever faced isn't enough. We need authentic contact with nature and compassionate communication at the point of contact that will get at the heart of vulnerability. Most of our intimate experiences with nature are in zoos, parks, and aquariums, and Lertzman observed that when information on climate change was presented at these points of contact, resistance to the message was diminished.

What's happening here, in my mind, is empathy through shared experience—our ability to bridge the perception of self with the perception of others, and not just how we perceive them, but how they perceive themselves. It's the old saying of walking in someone else's shoes, or I suppose in the case of plants and animals, someone else's refuge or cage. Empathy isn't a magical gift we suddenly wake up with one day—it can be learned. When we have positive experiences with others, a learning mechanism is triggered in the brain that increases empathy and further, deeper engagement. It only takes a handful of these initial experiences for a person to make strong leaps toward empathic thinking and feeling.

But empathy is only the starting point. It alone isn't enough if we are to perform a miracle, that is, to become emotionally invested in the well-being of other lives that make up a thriving, biodiverse world. Empathy is simply a gateway to something more profound and life changing: compassion.

Empathy starts with seeing and experiencing the world through another's circumstances, beliefs, and life experiences. Compassion, on the other hand, is actually feeling, dealing with, accepting, and then acting based on that other's existence. Talk about making one's self vulnerable while taking on a good deal of complex emotion and thought. One way to build compassion is called metta meditation, where you repeat phrases out loud, phrases like "may you be happy and healthy and free of pain." These phrases are directed, quietly and to yourself, at those you witness who seem to be in distress. Barbara Fredrickson's study at the University of North Carolina showed that just seven weeks of metta practice helped participants increase life satisfaction and reduce depression. And more importantly, metta meditation leads to a decrease in bias toward others. While these studies focus on human-to-human contact, there's no reason why the contact can't be human to bird, bee, prairie dog, stone, or river. And when we start to invite all of the world into our lives in such a way, purposefully and on their own terms, we become ready to grow our compassion even more. Of course, that level of ethical thinking isn't so easy.

In their New York Times piece "The Arithmetic of Compassion," Scott and Paul Slovic point out that compassion lessens significantly as numbers go up; as in, when just one person is hurt compared to 14 people, or even one person compared to two, our ability to feel compassion diminishes. It's what they call "compassion fade" and "psychological numbing." Experiments bear out that donations of time and money shrink as the numbers of people affected rise. There's also something else called the "prominence effect":

> [It] explains why genuinely well-meaning people (and their governments) so often fail to intervene to prevent genocides and other large-scale abuses. "Prominent" actions or objectives are those that are easily justified, though they may not match our stated social values. For example: decisions that protect national security or satisfy our attachment to near-term comforts and conveniences are easily justified. Such choices, as Paul Slovic explains in a recent *University of Illinois Law Review* article, are likely to trump decisions to protect people or the environment, especially when the humans in need or the environmental phenomena in jeopardy (species, habitats, the planet's climate) are so vast in scale as to seem distant and abstract.

Slovic and Slovic go on to cite the work of psychologist Robert Ornstein and biologist Paul Ehrlich, who argued decades ago that our brains have not kept up with modern problems of a global scale—phenomena like nuclear war or climate change. What they call for is a conscious evolution or an intentional change in how we think, process, and respond to these new realities.

I'll go ahead and argue that conscious evolution starts in two places that must be equal, as they are intertwined: the heart and the mind. We need gut checks. We need deep emotional experiences that so often start with touch, sight, and sound. Couple these sensations and experiences with learned knowledge from science and even philosophy and art and the depth of our emotional response can become more visceral and powerful. Our compassion can meet the needed revolution of our species in a human-made world. We need to feel deeply, and we need to think deeply. We need to be tested, torn apart, and made vulnerable.

The Benedictine monk Thomas Merton describes that sweeping vulnerability in his always clear and emotive language: "The whole idea of compassion is based on a keen awareness of the interdependence of all these living beings, which are all part of one another, and all involved in one another." Merton's compassion is an ethical and even a moral one, a selfless and actionable compassion that confronts, accepts, and transforms our agonies, grief, and doubts into passionate reconciliation. Such an act takes a great amount of courage and love. Caring for others is a highly evolved way of caring for the self, and this is how our landscapes need to change.

As we lose species and places, as we lose the safety nets of biodiversity and relatively predictable natural patterns, grief is our normal and fundamental response. Elisabeth Kubler-Ross's five stages of grief may help us understand and work through environmental grief—an emotion that can quite easily prevent us from healing ourselves and those around us, miring us in agony that could manifest itself in outward violence. Kubler-Ross created her model of grief while studying terminally ill patients, which seems to align perfectly with our new global reality.

The five stages—denial, anger, bargaining, depression, and acceptance—aren't necessarily sequential, but they can be. It makes some sense that these stages could occur in the above order, yet grief is complex—each person's responses and process in dealing with it so individualized—that there's no predictable norm. But one universal reality is that avoiding or minimizing our emotions will prolong grief, and this is something I see in the garden world quite clearly.

I see this sidestepping of grief when we avoid confronting how gardens collectively and meaningfully impact the environment.

We'll defend our plant and design choices to the last. We'll point to policies and the difficulty of changing them, or we will accept those policies, arguing that they must be good for something or they wouldn't exist. We'll diminish someone's point of view by saying it's already been said. We'll argue that someone's words could have been said better so as to be more appealing instead of addressing the core meaning of those words head on. We'll use labels to dismiss ideas that call into question or challenge systems of power that bring us comfort and give our assumptions credence in an uncertain world we want to make ordered and predictable. We will do anything we can to avoid looking more deeply and authentically at our culture so we don't have to face the loss, the grief, and the effort to change or be agents of change in a world crying out for compassion on a profound new level. Ironically, the profound new level is one gardeners regularly experience or at least dabble with every day.

Mary Pipher describes this avoidance of processing grief in her environmental psychology book *The Green Boat*: "We humans are programmed to respond to threats by fleeing or fighting. Our global storm will not let us do either. Our problems feel too big to fight and there is no place we can flee to, so we feel paralyzed. We are in a crisis that is too scary to confront and too important to ignore. Willful ignorance occurs when it feels wrong to acknowledge and wrong not to acknowledge a situation. This leads to crazy-making attempts to balance precariously between awareness and denial." Native plants are important, we may all agree, but they are not important enough to change our beliefs and ideals that a garden is primarily art or a place solely for human enjoyment. Even when scientific evidence showing the interconnectedness of native plants and wildlife is well-known, we're slow to augment our concepts of garden making, or to evolve our sense of ethics beyond our immediate social and cultural preconceptions. Gardens composed of both native and exotic plants constitute a precarious balance between awareness and denial of our environmental impact, and are a simultaneous safeguard against our grief overwhelming us.

Years ago, I stumbled upon photographs of Laysan albatross on Midway Atoll, where the birds gather and nest. The images showed decomposing bodies at various stages, but most often just feather and bone. Where the birds' bellies used to be were collections of colorful plastic—cigarette lighters, doll shoes, toothbrushes, bottle caps, and torn pieces from who knows what. Through the albatross images, I learned of the Great Pacific Garbage Patch, a floating debris field the size of Texas and growing exponentially. It's a region in the middle of the ocean that currents circle around, leaving a relatively calm center where debris blown from cargo ships or family picnics eventually finds its way. Over decades, the plastic in this debris field will disintegrate, but never totally vanish, becoming small enough to enter the food chain. In fact, we eat plastic every day as it breaks down into smaller and smaller microscopic fragments. Unfortunately, the Great Pacific Garbage Patch is just one of many across the world's oceans.

I recently read more about the albatross photographer Chris Jordan and his experiences with a near-paralyzing grief he suffered on Midway day after day. "I discovered that grief is not the same as sadness and despair," he begins, going on to say that it is not a debilitating feeling to be avoided at all costs. "Grief is the same as love. Grief is a felt experience of love for something that we're losing, or that we've lost…the role of the artist is not to relieve us of feelings of hopelessness, despair, rage, or love, but to help us feel those things." In 2009 the American Psychological Association convened a task force to explore why people aren't acting in the face of climate change. They discovered that a primary way to avoid dealing with the reality was to face it only intellectually, without emotions playing any key role. It's a sort of mental gymnastics we all perform to circumvent the full impact and destruction we're having on the natural world, the real world, just like the way Pacific ocean currents move around the Great Garbage Patch as it builds, and builds, and builds.

In the same article on Chris Jordan, the author, Brooke Jarvis, calls out what's going on: namely, that hopelessness is an "intolerable bogeyman to be kept away with the right incantation." Jordan elucidates on this reality by saying, "you acknowledge the presence of darkness...we have this cultural obsession with hope, I'm not sure how useful hope really is." When someone asks Jordan at a presentation what they can do about the albatross on Midway, he says that person "may be feeling something uncomfortable that they don't want to feel. They're feeling the enormity and the complexity of the problems of our world, and that makes them feel anxious." There's no easy answer to give them, he admits, because providing one would be "like pulling the plug in a bathtub: the feeling all drains out. My job is to help people connect with what they feel, even if it's uncomfortable."

It's okay, and even necessary, to feel bad about our role in environmental destruction. Our culture tells us not to feel bad, that there's something wrong with you if you're depressed, angry, upset, or even feel "negative" emotions deeply. And we repeat this message to each other, even to ourselves. Maybe this avoidance of heavy emotions is why we distrust or feel alienated by activists, even going so far as to call them terrorists. What our culture does not tell us is that feeling bad can be a necessary step toward unprecedented change, empowerment, and freedom. Here's author Joanna Macy on learning to embrace challenging emotions:

> None of us, in our hearts, is free of sorrow for the suffering of other beings. None of us is indifferent to the dangers that threaten our planet's people, or free of fear for the generations to come. Yet when we are enjoined to "keep smiling," "be sociable," and "keep a stiff upper lip," it is not easy to give credence to this anguish.... Suppression of our natural responses to actual or impending disaster is part of the disease of our time, as Robert Jay Lifton, the American psychiatrist who pioneered the study of the psychological effects of nuclear bombs, explains. The refusal to acknowledge or experience these responses produces a profound and dangerous splitting. It divorces our mental calculations from our intuitive, emotional, and biological imbeddedness in the matrix of life.

I'm not advocating wallowing in the muck and mire of agony. I'm advocating for the freedom to feel wholly and without hindrance the emotional reality of our situation. Embedded in that reality is an unstoppable force that profiteering corporations and the elected officials they own—not to mention every consumer-based commercial on television—doesn't want you to access. It's okay to feel bad. It's okay to feel. It's okay to think critically. It's okay to doubt. It's okay to be so angry you step up to the plate and live the dream of a better world, an honorable world, a just world for all species forever.

We avoid anger and sadness as if they are deadly diseases. Yet we can't open ourselves to liberating realizations and empowerment if we're afraid of knowledge or connection. I feel rage at our complicity in extinction. I feel deep sorrow and almost break into tears. The same rage and sadness I feel reading reports from the front lines of gun violence is the same wonder and awe I feel watching a caterpillar eat a leaf; they are all the same emotions that can't be individually cherry-picked to save my ego or preserve the illusion of my privileged human culture. I need anger. I need sadness. I need awe. I need to be humbled so that I am part of the world again—so that I can fight the systems of denial and oppression. I also need hopelessness because, as philosopher and cultural critic Derrick Jensen asserts, "hope is a longing for a future condition over which you have no agency; it means you are essentially powerless."

How can we heal if we don't feel to the core? It's not our fault that we feel bad, yet we internalize and store these quiet feelings to the point of tacitly accepting our grief instead of dealing with it. We tend to cover up this grief, psychologist David Kidner says, by calling it depression, some clinical condition to be neatly categorized. Then we treat it with medication and therapy to silence the feelings. I'm not talking here of those who have diagnosed and life-threatening chemical imbalances, but I am addressing a Western culture that prizes spinning anything "negative" into something more happy without fully processing our emotional situation.

In a *New York Times* piece, Gabriele Oettingen, professor of psychology at New York University, discusses why positive thinking might not be so beneficial:

> Many people think that the key to success is to cultivate and doggedly maintain an optimistic outlook. But the truth is that positive thinking often hinders us.... Why doesn't positive thinking work the way you might assume? As my colleagues and I have discovered, dreaming about the future calms you down, measurably reducing systolic blood pressure, but it also can drain you of the energy you need to take action in pursuit of your goals. Positive thinking fools our minds into perceiving that we've already attained our goal, slackening our readiness to pursue it.
>
> Some critics of positive thinking have advised people to discard all happy talk and "get real" by dwelling on the challenges or obstacles. But this is too extreme a correction. Studies have shown that this strategy doesn't work any better than entertaining positive fantasies. What does work better is a hybrid approach that combines positive thinking with "realism." Here's how it works. Think of a wish. For a few minutes, imagine the wish coming true, letting your mind wander and drift where it will. Then shift gears. Spend a few more minutes imagining the obstacles that stand in the way of realizing your wish.

The spin to the happy and the avoidance of "negative" emotions creates another tool by which we can avoid working through the stages of grief. You'll see it in the response of some who say to stop wagging your finger, to not be so judgmental, to not be so critical when advocating for something like native plants or gardens that aren't just for humans. In the end it's the critical thinking we might be running from, the act of calling us all out in our shared, collective problems we know exist but find hard to address. If we look at the science of native plants and the science of extinction and climate change, the trail leads us to stark realizations about the choices we make in our landscapes, as well as the entire garden of Earth. If we have only positive emotional connections with the species we choose to connect with—species obvious in our environment, like robins and squirrels—we tacitly choose to deny other lives, like spiders, ants, and wasps, that are fundamental to the landscape. It can be easy to divorce ourselves from the world in subtle, accumulative ways.

Another defensive thought process might now be circling the wagons: "Stop shaming us." But it's not shame. It may be guilt, but it's not shame. Exploring the reality of the world we've altered is not shameful. It's a practice in empathy and compassion on an order we have either lost over time or are unwilling or unable to foster.

Jennifer Jacquet in her book *Is Shame Necessary?* differentiates between shame and guilt, and the constructive uses for both on environmental issues within specific groups and circumstances. She defines shame as a way to hold individuals to a group standard. It's a way to regulate personal behavior by threatening more extreme retribution (think Nathaniel Hawthorne's *The Scarlet Letter*). By contrast, guilt holds individuals to their own standard. If you feel guilty about something, it's likely that you've broken your own ethical or moral code—and maybe you've been called out on it. Our Western culture prizes the individual, compared to, for example, many Asian cultures that are based on large social collectives, and so in the West, guilt is more prevalent and preferable to shame. And for Western cultures, guilt is an emotional and modern construct created by an individualistic society.

Jacquet contends this: "Shame is not only a feeling. It's also a tool—a delicate and sometimes dangerous one—that we can put to use to help solve serious problems. Shaming is a nonviolent form of resistance that anyone can use, and, unlike guilt, it can be used to influence the way groups behave—shame can scale." She sees shame as an ideal instrument to expose a minority of players who are doing something unethical. For example, we all use plastics and we should understand the repercussions of living in a plasticized culture, and once we understand those repercussions, we will make an ethical choice on how to respond. If we all agree that plastic is harmful to the environment, shame can be used to call out groups—like businesses and cities—to affect change.

And this is where the wool has been pulled over our eyes in a society that puts the economy before the living world. Corporations play into our guilt as consumers, helping us assuage that guilt by buying the so-called right products: dolphin-free tuna, recycled paper, responsibly tested cosmetics, GMO-free cereal, pesticide-free flowers, et cetera. But consumers only make decisions as individuals apart from the larger group, Jacquet says, which shows guilt's power is limited. It can even be used by those in power to discourage a group from demanding more powerful changes, or from using shame to do so. Our individual choices aren't enough, especially if we aren't making them as part of a larger group consciousness that's demanding positive, systemic environmental change. Jacquet continues, "The fact that shame is so bound to the norm also means we should not blame shame—the emotion or the act of shaming—for making us uncomfortable if what we actually disagree with is the norm that shame is attempting to enforce." In other words, when we demand that others stop making us feel guilty or shameful, it's not the individual we're trying to silence, it's the larger cultural and social systems we're trying to normalize or tacitly reinforce.

My thoughts gravitate toward women's, LGBT, and black rights activist Audre Lorde, who exclaims: "I cannot hide my anger to spare you guilt, nor hurt feelings, nor answering anger; for to do so insults and trivializes all our efforts. Guilt is not a response to anger; it is a response to one's own actions or lack of action. If it leads to change then it can be useful, since it is then no longer guilt but the beginning of knowledge." For Lorde, who is responding to critics of her own vocal and passionate activism, we can't sidestep the profound moral issues we have to address if we're to evolve socially. The choices we make in life are evidence of our ethics, and our ethics continually need to be tested, re-evaluated, and reshaped. In a world of rapid climate change and mass extinction, we may find that our ethics need to be redefined more often than our culture and economic systems can handle. And as our ethics evolve, our gardens need to evolve along with them.

As we dig deeper into how we respond to perceived threats to our beliefs, we're practicing critical thinking. It's not the same as being critical or criticizing someone on a personal level, nor is it a process to attain personal pleasure from making an opposing argument. The success of freedom and democracy, and the extent to which we help other species and places practice these inalienable rights, is based on how well we think beyond the surface of our culture and our genetic hardwiring. It's what scientists Robert Ornstein and Paul Ehrlich propose, that we need to force our own evolution to catch up with our planet-wide crises. But we now live in a culture where critical thinking—calling into question assumed beliefs and the status quo given to us by those in power—is demonized. A culture where activism is seen as terrorism and knowledge is distrusted if we disagree with it.

A thoughtful opinion piece by author Greg Lukianoff and psychologist Jonathan Haidt appeared in *The Atlantic*, titled "The Coddling of the American Mind." The authors explore how free speech and critical thinking in our universities and colleges is being undermined by the phenomenon of trigger warnings, a practice wherein professors and others forewarn students that books, lectures, films, and other experiences may trigger a form of post-traumatic stress disorder that makes students uncomfortable. The concept of trigger warnings is not an idea to be dismissed, especially as they are designed to protect those who have experienced previous physical or emotional trauma. During my years of university teaching, I had plenty of students come to me after class or during office hours—sometimes even in class discussion—who shared their stories of abuse, rape, depression, chemical dependence, and more, seeking my advice and help on how to deal with them in the face of challenging texts that brought difficult experiences back to the surface.

I don't pretend to be a psychologist or therapist, but many times I had to simulate one as a professor, and the best way to do so was to listen. The second-best way was to ask questions that helped the student explore, confront, and process their emotions. We often did so by writing personal essays, which afforded us the time to carefully consider how our lives, our emotions, and our responses were empowering and life-changing, and could even help others who read or heard about them. Working through these responses is no easy thing at any age. Time and again I saw the student with the most resistance and doubt become the most vulnerable, and in turn write the truest, most affecting sentences of their lives. Perhaps when we tune into our fears and preconceptions, we can, at least some of the time, come to know ourselves and our world more authentically and more powerfully. Maybe this is where radical activism begins. Just as we need nature to punch us in the gut, we may need our ethical ideologies to do the same.

The recent trend of trigger warnings noted by the authors of *The Atlantic* piece, however—a trend that is taking place across college campuses as well as within our larger culture—exploits the intended use of trigger warnings to instead silence those who offer a different perspective. This exploitation labels anything that challenges us or makes us feel uncomfortable as not just troubling, but wrong. Lukianoff and Haidt state that policing speech is "likely to engender patterns of thought that are surprisingly similar to those long identified by cognitive behavioral therapists as causes of depression and anxiety. The new protectiveness may be teaching students to think pathologically.... A recent study shows that implicit or unconscious biases are now at least as strong across political parties as they are across races."

They continue their argument by making this illuminating summary:

So it's not hard to imagine why students arriving on campus today might be more desirous of protection and more hostile toward ideological opponents than in generations past. This hostility, and the self-righteousness fueled by strong partisan emotions, can be expected to add force to any moral crusade. A principle of moral psychology is that "morality binds and blinds." Part of what we do when we make moral judgments is express allegiance to a team. But that can interfere with our ability to think critically.

How can we think critically, then, when we are trying to cultivate a moral response to perceived threats and crises? How can we precisely guide our passionate emotions to a constructive action that doesn't alienate, but liberates us from destructive behavior? Anyone with a strong passion or opinion is automatically labeled as an extremist, self-righteous, holier-than-thou, or close-minded—and in the human-only world, this might more often than not be a generally fair diagnosis. But what happens when we enter the nonhuman world, when we advocate for equality and understanding across species, or for a morality or ethics based on the lives of other creatures? Are we able to extend empathy beyond ourselves? Compassion? Gardening with native plants isn't demonstrating bigotry by excluding plants from Asia, and it's no more "ideological" than gardening with a mix of plants or 100 percent exotics or plastic tulips, as my grandmother did beneath a shady portico.

I am passionate about native plants, and I know our built landscapes are doing far more harm than they have to—not only measurable harm to water quality, unneeded energy use, and lack of wildlife habitat, but psychological harm that distances us from our homes. I'm angry. I'm full of despair. But anger and despair can be rooted in compassion. Emotions frequently labeled as negative, something to run away from, can be more than simply powerful physical tools. They can reshape our ethical framework. What is sacred in our lives and our world? What do we fight for and how far will we go? How easy it is to slip into stagnation, to not care too much because it's easier on our hearts and minds, when caring can open us to the wounded nature of our world, not only making us part of the wounding, but also part of the healing. We are bound to the places we call home in ways we are afraid to confess or embrace, but we must, and in full force. Author Joy Williams' words bear repeating: "The ecological crisis cannot be resolved by politics. It cannot be resolved by science or technology. It is a crisis caused by culture and character, and a deep change in personal consciousness is needed.... This is essentially a moral issue we face, and moral decisions must be made."

So how can we openly and honestly practice a critical thought process that exposes our biases and assumptions while facilitating meaningful change on a global scale? Philosophers have long espoused that we don't see life for what it is but only our distorted version of it, a version colored by hopes, fears, and upbringing. How can we detach ourselves from ourselves, so to speak, if we're to get at our true selves in the context of all life on Earth and how we impact that life?

The practice that can help us overcome our biases is something called cognitive behavioral therapy, the most extensively studied non-pharmaceutical treatment of mental illness. It is used widely to treat depression, anxiety, addiction, and more. Cognitive behavioral therapy has been found to be as effective as antidepressant drugs for treating anxiety and depression, and the therapy is rather simple, with far-lasting effects that never end—precisely because it teaches people new ways to think. Again, from Lukianoff and Haidt's piece:

> The goal is to minimize distorted thinking and see the world more accurately. You start by learning the names of the dozen or so most common cognitive distortions (such as overgeneralizing, discounting positives, and emotional

reasoning...). Each time you notice yourself falling prey to one of them, you name it, describe the facts of the situation, consider alternative interpretations, and then choose an interpretation of events more in line with those facts. Your emotions follow your new interpretation. In time, this process becomes automatic. When people improve their mental hygiene in this way—when they free themselves from the repetitive irrational thoughts that had previously filled so much of their consciousness—they become less depressed, anxious, and angry.

How can we apply cognitive behavioral therapy to our thinking about the environment and urban wildlife gardens? We have to recognize that our thinking is distorted. Our culture prizes the rights of the individual over those of the group, or even of other individuals. When someone presents another point of view that seems to challenge our individual rights, which makes us feel guilty, we tend to jerk our knees. Recall that guilt is a personal emotion, a triggered response of an individual understanding that their own action goes against their conception of right. Responses to a native plant proponent might be to overgeneralize the argument, discount the positives of native plants, assume knowledge of the other's motivations or thoughts without allowing explanation, applying a reductive label to the native plant proponent as a way to dismiss their concerns, blame the other perspective for your negative feelings, or create hypothetical situations that exacerbate the tension instead of working to fully address the issue.

Mary Pipher again gets to the psychological heart of our responses to protect ourselves from too much environmental reality. People might do any one of the following:
1. Deny reality entirely
2. Accept some aspect of reality but deny other equally critical aspects
3. Minimize or normalize
4. Overemphasize our lack of power

5. Deny their emotional investment in reality
6. Compartmentalize
7. Feign apathy
8. Kill the messenger

Pipher asserts that "psychological research on cognitive dissonance shows that the more profound the threat the more rigorously it is denied." How often does this happen when we discuss climate change, even as almost every scientist agrees we're causing it? Or when we add evidence from mass extinction? How often does this happen during what too quickly become heated debates about the efficacy of native plants beyond serving humans alone? Far too frequently, we allow personal perspectives based on invested social backgrounds to dominate a collective good we all probably agree on, at least inherently. As Pipher ultimately states, "in recent years, many pragmatic problems—fluoridation, conservation, immigration, and climate change—have been recategorized as political ones. Our country's polarization around ideologies has distorted issues and made fixing many problems impossible." How do we find a common ground when our passions, and the fixed reality those passions are grounded on, define how we interact with the world?

I've experienced plenty of overly militant native plant proponents—and at times, I confess I've let my passion get the best of me. But I won't apologize for the root of that passion—my belief that gardens matter in profound social, cultural, and ethical ways that will shape our response to climate change and extinction, and the social justice issues they call up, like classism and racism. Our built landscapes should be as close to 100 percent native plants as possible, and achieving this goal is logistically, practically, and economically viable in every way we can imagine. Even so, native plant landscapes, and the critical and ethical thinking they ask of us, are difficult for the very reason that they ask us to bring other species into our lives, seemingly displacing ourselves and our accustomed or privileged beliefs.[2]

Perhaps our landscapes too often practice a sort of speciesism. In that way, they may even embody the worst of what we do to ourselves and each other—marginalization, possession, and superiority. We use our landscapes to divide and conquer the world, instead of learning to understand it and becoming a meaningful part of it. Here's author and activist Terry Tempest Williams:

> Most people are not comfortable making a connection between racism and speciesism or the ill treatment of human beings and the mistreatment of animals. We want to keep our boundaries clean and separate. But isn't that the point, to separate, isolate, and discriminate? We create hierarchies, viewing life from the top down, top being, of course, God, then a ranking of human races, and so our judgments move down "the Great Chain of Being" until we touch rocks. This is the attitude of power, and it hinges on who is in control. Who has power over whom? How does this kind of behavior infiltrate the psyche of a culture? And what are the consequences of scala natura?.... Arrogance is arrogance, and cruelty committed to a person or an animal is cruelty. We would rather not think too much about "what is being done to those outside the sphere of the favored group," yet I believe it is time in the evolution of our imagination to make a strong case for the extension of our empathy toward the Other.

Our gardens are places of arrogance and alienation. We are a species very much alone in the world, trying to find an intimate, stabilizing connection we once had with other species. But somehow we are unable to give ourselves to the rather simple communication of empathy, compassion, and shared fate. In our gardens, we may show the greatest alienation, placing plants how and where we want and using species unrecognizable to wildlife. In our gardens, then, is arrogance—that we matter more, that our passions and loves, our losses and agonies, are separate and even superior to those of other species. While our gardens could ideally function as bridges between our world and the worlds of an infinite number of lives, too often they are walls of hubris and human-made disorder we impose upon a world already ordered to maximum benefit through millions of years of trial and error. What we wish to improve upon may be our own human-made alienation as creatures who struggle with an ethics that must encompass not just different races and creeds, but also animals, plants, and fungi. In a world of climate change and mass extinction, intimate gardens out our back door might be the best places to generate a landscape ethic that evolves into an activist-based global ethic of creation care for all life.

CHAPTER 4

Urban Wildness and Social Justice

A "post-wild" world would put
human civilization into a kind of
solitary confinement. There would
be no away, no frontier or edge
to civilization. There would be no
other, nothing to contest our will.
We would be left all alone.

— JASON MARK

No CONVERSATION can become more heated than the one
about how we use our landscapes. I know this fact first-
hand from living in a state where some 85 percent of rural land is
privately owned and folks are wary of any perceived government
interference, whether in the form of water use regulations, endangered species acts, or taxes. Our culture romanticizes aspects of
farming, especially the idea that all of those cornfields are feeding
the world. But in reality, most of the corn produced in the United
States does not go to human consumption. Instead, 40 percent
goes into the energy-intensive production of ethanol and another
45 percent is fed to animals. The romantic or mythical tradition
of land ownership, and the freedom or right to do with that land
as one pleases, extends into urban and suburban land use as well.
If you want to start a spirited conversation on landscape design

and land use as communal, suggest to someone that they shouldn't plant Asian butterfly bush (*Buddleja davidii*).

The reasons for the butterfly bush debate extend far deeper than exotic versus native.[1] The shrub benefits from a well-chosen common name, which implies it is a butterfly magnet and thus an important plant to include in pollinator and wildlife gardens. Indeed, it does attract butterflies, most especially the large charismatic ones we love to see—swallowtails, monarchs, and their ilk. You'll also see occasional smaller butterflies visiting, as well as bumble bees with tongues long enough to reach the nectar. However, most pollinating insects have tongues too short to get nectar from this plant, so they prefer the more accessible pollen of shallow ray flowers. And what insect uses butterfly bush as a host plant here in North America? Not one. Without larvae, there can be no adults, and without plants that provide more than one ecosystem service, we aren't gardening smarter, and we aren't helping as much as we'd like to believe.

But there's the rub: that we help, must help, should help. We're told—and so we believe—that for wildlife to fare well, we have to intervene. This natural urge toward empathy often compels us to act in ways that might ultimately harm wildlife. Butterfly bush is an aggressive plant, one that grows out of brick walls in England and along road edges and in open fields in the eastern United States and Appalachia. A few Pacific Northwest states have banned its import and sale for these very reasons. Despite evidence of the plant's aggressive tendencies in parts of the US, gardeners in the Midwest tend to argue that planting butterfly bush in their ecoregions is not a problem, as they don't witness it spreading in their landscapes. What this argument overlooks, however, is that birds are the primary dispersers of its seeds, which they can spread far and wide. As the climate warms, this large plant will change ecosystems like so many others before it. To combat butterfly bush's tendency to spread, new "sterile" versions are being cultivated. One problem is that over time cultivars can revert to their origins. After all, a plant's main objective is to find a way to overcome, reproduce, and survive. In the attempt to justify our plant choices, to have

what we want regardless of what the environment may want or
need, we go far in altering life to fit our purposes.

We've remade our world and, admittedly, have done so for a
long time. One example is the Plains tribes of North America who
set fire to grasslands to produce rich new growth, which attracted
foraging bison herds. Human interaction with the natural world in
this example, however, did not operate at the same level at which
humans are currently shaping the world. We have intensified and
expedited the processes by which we exploit the natural world for
human benefit with little regard for nonhuman life. Our lives are
easier the higher we place ourselves and our desires above all else—
I know this by visiting the grocery store at 2 AM and buying fruit
out of season, or running my air conditioner instead of changing
into a more lightweight shirt. Earth is novel now, a combination
of innate wildness and the evidence of our reshaping or eradicating that wildness. How well and how quickly the Earth's species
respond to human-induced changes, and how or if we redefine our
role as one species among many, will determine our legacy for the
rest of geologic time.

Living with the world in a better way often gets boiled down
to either changing light bulbs and recycling, or conserving and
restoring landscapes to preserve our idea of untouched wildness
and ecosystem or ecological function. But the very term "ecosystem
or ecological function" carries cold, unfeeling shades of meaning;
we're simply trying to quantify in black and white the benefits of
a landscape. How we measure those benefits and for whom are
important considerations, because it's often from the perspective of one species: ours. How much human-caused change can
a place withstand until its self-sustaining wildness can no longer
function to filter the water or clean the air or create rich soil or
provide usable habitat? How far can we go—and even when we
go too far, can we just change the wordage or the definitions so
it appears we're still doing okay? For example, instead of pushing for "native plants," for fear the term might irk some folks, we
instead say "native and adapted," thereby insinuating we're still
making wholesome landscapes choices even if we're using lots of

non-native plants that wildlife can't recognize and that may only provide nectar for competitive, generalist pollinators. Changing our language is one way we justify the idea that all plants play a positive ecological role in our gardens, when what we're really trying to do is not ruffle any feathers or give ourselves permission to carry on changing the world as we see fit. We can look to biologist Doug Tallamy and plantsman Rick Darke for guidance on how to define our current urban world's penchant for avoiding the deeper, necessary conversation in garden design:

> The relationship between landscaping practices and the production of vital ecosystem services has created ethical issues never before faced by gardeners. Because the resources and services that support all humans come from functional landscapes, and function starts with plants, the planting and management choices we make at home impact our neighbors and indeed, our greater society as a whole. In essence, the relationship between plants and ecosystem function makes the ecological functionality in our landscapes a public resource, just like a reservoir, a river, and a national park. Unfortunately, this new reality is in direct conflict with Western culture's tradition of private land ownership.

Think about gardens as a public resource for a moment. Isn't that concept wholly against the grain of our Western society based on the individual's rights? Our home landscapes are places where we can exercise our free will and, in some ways, impose our own idea of perfection on an imperfect landscape. But when we don't see our landscapes as part of a common good, or as part of a living democracy for humans and more, we threaten the values we hold most dear—such as health, freedom, and compassion. These values are also threatened when we, mixing plants with no shared evolutionary history with one another or the local fauna, create novel ecosystems.

We can also look to Tallamy and Darke for a definition of what a novel environment or ecosystem is:

85% of the earth's ecosystems are now novel, containing species with no prior history of interaction and no evolutionary relationship. Such ecosystems are built, at least in part, from non-relational biodiversity. A linguist could successfully argue that, without functional interactions, such collections of organisms do not constitute an ecosystem at all.

Ecosystems with living components that can't relate to one another are ecosystems that don't thrive. And they certainly don't make significant inroads helping species adapt to climate change or, perhaps, escape extinction. We need to ask ourselves how every plant is contributing to the rich language of the garden—not just the visual aesthetic but also the much more valuable and central underlying languages that time has forged among insects, beetles, spiders, and birds. For example, what species use butterfly bush and why? What happens to an environment when it begins to spread outside of its planted landscape? Who uses daffodils or daylily as a host plant, and what wildlife are using them for nectar, pollen, nesting material, et cetera? Will species that can't use these plants soon evolve or adapt to be able to use them? What's happening below the soil line? What larger ecological niche are the plants filling? How are the plants influencing nearby evolution of the ecosystem? What viable ecological relationships does a Russian sage have when placed next to a butterfly milkweed?

We practice making novel ecosystems every day without a very good understanding of what we're doing or how ecosystems work in clear detail. While Tallamy and Darke say 85 percent of the world is novel, other studies show current levels at 36 percent. University of Victoria ecologist Eric Higgs describes what a novel ecosystem is by defining three levels of landscape: historical (wild) ecosystems that show no or little change, hybrid (mostly wild) ecosystems that show reversible changes, and novel ecosystems.

The last shows irreversible changes with a radical difference from historical ecosystem structure, composition, and function, and an ongoing self-organization that's either human created or self created. A novel ecosystem, then, is one that's been so totally altered from its original state that there's no hope for it to return to that state; even if you tried to restore it, it would still revert to a state of novelty.

A few questions that have long riled conservationists include the following. How do we know what a place looked like before it changed? When did the change occur? How can we even hope to understand all of its ecological nuances—especially if no current example exists? Additionally, do the wildlife that once used the environment still exist in this place, and to what degree? What is their importance? With these questions in mind, I think about prairie and in particular its soils, which harbored unique bacteria that may have facilitated plant growth or aided in nutrient exchanges or performed any number of other services. And while the surface of an ecosystem might appear healthy and stable, the soil composition or water features below ground (the hydrology) may be changing. In our gardens, let alone our public parks and rights of way, how do we know we're achieving our aims? How can we make the novel nature of cities work for us and for other local species? How can we foster wildlife while helping it evolve or adapt, if that is even possible? What benefits can expanding wildness offer in a world facing climate change and mass extinction?

We imagine wildness to be "out there," somewhere far from us, protected and fairly pristine. We make pilgrimages to nature and take pretty pictures, then come back to our alienated lives watching Saturday afternoon nature specials and Disney movies. Conservationists have long sought to preserve and restore wildness in those "out there" places, often seen as repositories for biodiversity, armored safes where wildness can do its thing unencumbered by too much direct influence from us. But our clogged roads through Yellowstone tell a different tale, as do 406 ppm of atmospheric CO_2 that touches every last square inch under the waves, on land,

and in the air. And yet, it's these places we visit that foster our urge to help. And help them we must, so whatever bit of wildness that remains might be able to change and adapt. A joint World Wildlife Fund and London Zoological Society analysis of 3,700 species with sufficient data shows that, on average, vertebrate species have lost nearly 60 percent of their numbers since 1970. How do we conserve and restore? Do we even try?

Peter Kareiva, senior science advisor to the Nature Conservancy's president and director of the Institute of the Environment and Sustainability at UCLA, says that when an ecosystem is altered at any level it is gone forever—so we need to accept this and move on because, in reality, there is no pristine nature and no way to measure it. Kareiva's viewpoint is one shared by a new group of ecologists who are often dubbed either modernist greens or ecopragmatists. Their perspective tends to be optimistic; viewing nature as resilient and able to heal itself, with some constructive help from humans. Novel ecosystems are here to stay, they profess, and there's little reason to feel bad or worried about them because nature will endure long after we are gone. But this kind of thinking is problematic.

In many ways, Kareiva and the ecopragmatists are responding emotionally to what most perceive as the burdensome doom-and-gloom rhetoric of climate change and mass extinction. An optimistic response is both relevant and inevitable. We've always put our faith in the Earth, in its systems and its ability to be there for us no matter what, which is why we so often call it "mother." If Earth isn't there for us, if its systems aren't self-perpetuating and repairable in a time frame that benefits us, much of our epistemology—how we view ourselves as a society—begins to shatter. We lose our faith. But as explored in the previous chapter, the healthiest response to our crises may be to confront them brutally and honestly, without spinning or doctoring to make us feel temporarily better. It's important to note again the thoughts of Eric Higgs, coauthor of the book *Novel Ecosystems: Intervening in the New Ecological World Order*, who cautions against assuming novel ecosystems are beneficial, even if they perform some ecosystem services. What they supplant is likely to have been far more beneficial because that landscape evolved to suit the place over a long time frame, with various species carving out niches where all available resources were captured and cycled in the landscape.

Daniel Simberloff, professor in the Department of Ecology and Evolutionary Biology at the University of Tennessee, decries the idea that novel ecosystems are so inevitable that they are the new normal. He points out that we have no criteria to show how an ecosystem is novel or what thresholds it reaches to be labeled as novel—not to mention that ecosystems are constantly changing, influenced by humans or not. Simberloff goes on to say, quite truthfully, that modern restoration ecology does not "attempt to recreate the past; rather, the goal is to re-establish the historical trajectory of an ecosystem before anthropogenic influences derailed it." In other words, the aim is not ecological restoration but ecological revival. There hasn't been one time when I advocated for native plants in garden landscapes that someone hasn't been critical of my "silly" attempt to return to some mythical, puritan, idealistic past. But I wouldn't want to go back; the bucolic concept of perfect, unspoiled nature fueled a Western manifest destiny that all but destroyed entire cultures of plant, animal, and Native American societies. There is no unspoiled nature. There is only us in a world we garden for the good of all of us, or for the good of just some of us. We either take the long view or the short view. We either privilege ourselves now at the expense of those who come after, or we privilege those who come after while reviving our current world.

Siberloff makes one final point: "There is no evidence that any particular ecosystem cannot be restored in the sense of modern restoration ecology; the impediments are economic and political, not scientific or technological. This does not imply that society should undertake to restore every ecosystem; each case should be considered by all stakeholders in terms of desirability, cost, and resource availability." As climates move some 360 feet each year—as novel ecosystems are created—we need criteria to measure them on a case by case basis, and we need historic baselines to measure them against. It seems an almost impossible task both logistically and financially, requiring experts from a plethora of fields and regions; perhaps we need to start measuring now, since the world will look significantly different in just a few years.

But let's take a step back. Species evolve, right? Even if ecosystems become so altered by humans that they can't perform historic levels of ecosystem function, new species will naturally evolve and the Earth will heal itself, one argument goes. Well, it takes millennia or tens of millennia for one new species to evolve, while vast numbers die out in the same time frame because they cannot adapt. Living in such a species-deficient world would be psychologically detrimental, and not just because we'd have fewer oranges to choose from and unsafe water or soil. We are forcing new species to appear through unnatural selection in the form of domesticated animals and plants, genetic modification, hunting, deforestation, overfishing, suburbanization, and more, according to a study published in the *Proceedings of the Royal Society B*. The study's coauthor, Joseph Bull from the University of Copenhagen, states, "The prospect of artificially gaining novel species through human activities is unlikely to elicit the feeling that it can offset losses of natural species.... Indeed, many people might find the prospect of an artificially biodiverse world just as daunting as an artificially impoverished one." The real issue might not be how to make up for the lack of biodiversity we've forced upon many places, but how to stop interfering and let biodiversity find its way back. Our hand may already be too heavy.

In Chapter 2 we explored how weeds in urban centers are producing heavier seed to germinate in the same concrete cracks as the mother plant, and how swallows along I-80 in Nebraska have shorter wings to better dodge highway traffic. David Coltman, professor at the University of Alberta, and his colleagues have been following bighorn sheep on Ram Mountain just east of the Canadian Rockies for 40 years and are finding that, through hunting, the male sheep now have 25 percent shorter horns. That's not good news because larger horns help a ram compete for females, and it takes that ram years to grow its horns. But the crux, Coltman emphasizes, is that the horns are being harvested at legal lengths, but those lengths arrive well before rams can achieve social dominance to reproduce.

In the end, when we fish or hunt for sport, we aren't natural predators but tend to be relentless and efficient, often taking out the best animals. As we reshape entire environments through other alterations, we make changes on large scales that affect most everything, creating artificial selection without always knowing what the repercussions might be. For example, it takes on average one million years for a species to adapt to a single degree of temperature increase—so as we alter the climate, the novelty of the world shifts unpredictably, perhaps even unquantifiably.

Our gardens and managed landscapes provide us the opportunity to better understand our world, and to practice a more modern and adaptable version of conservation. Take, for example, the Nature Conservancy's Nebraska prairie manager Chris Helzer, whose ideas might be applied equally to large rural expanses and connected urban habitats. As Helzer puts forward, "If we're going to successfully restore the viability of fragmented prairies, we can't afford to waste time and effort worrying about whether or not we've matched pre-European settlement condition, or any other historical benchmark. Instead, we need to focus on patching the essential systems back together. After all, we're not building for the past, we're building for the future."

Helzer's words offer a bridge between embracing novel ecosystems and the efforts of old-school conservationists. Both have value, and both want the same ultimate outcome. And while Helzer is most certainly a native plant proponent in and beyond the prairie, he realizes that eliminating or even fighting some plants or systems isn't practical or affordable. But how we interpret these ideas and practices in our gardens is slightly more complicated than how we apply them to prairie expanses and can often become just as divisive, if not more so, when applied to individual landscapes.

Just as it's a challenge to define how novel an ecosystem is, as well as its potential benefits and drawbacks, we struggle to define the ecological value of our urban gardens. Gardens are naturally a nexus of ideology, and our Western tradition of gardens embraces cloistered refuges for the benefit of the few as well as idealized interpretations of nature more focused on art and human experience than on creating connective habitats or filtering stormwater. As much as the novel ecosystem and wildlife garden conversation is about fledgling new conservation science and urban aesthetics, it is also about ideology—and ethics. And ultimately it needs to be about all of the above at once, even if it makes us uncomfortable or is hard to wrap our heads around.

Where do our gardens come from, especially our concept of what they look like and what their purpose is?[2] It's important to at least briefly explore the foundation of Western design as this will help create a trajectory that redefines gardens for a new era. Our history of garden design is first, and maybe surprisingly, influenced by the Roman Empire, a culture that moved away from Greek-inspired landscapes of religious and spiritual ceremony. For the Romans, garden landscapes were about possession, status, and replicating scenes from myths and literature that, when copied throughout the empire, induced a sort of public order in tandem with their grid-patterned cities. This order was magnified by using garden spaces for public events such as oratory or theater performances. The focus was less on awe of nature and spiritual connectivity than on self-reliance and human reason.

Taking cues from formal Roman design, the cloistered gardens of medieval European monasteries were places of sheltered refuge from the violence and uncertainty of the time—a way to keep unfettered and dangerous nature at bay. Monks and privileged patrons could write their poetry or translate texts in the solitude, quiet, and peace behind the walls. These gardens were often punctuated by a central fountain in an open green, flower bed, or herb planting, which likely helped drown out noise while cooling the space in summer.

Toward the end of the fifteenth century the burgeoning Italian Renaissance began to combine elements of both Roman and cloistered design, in form and spirit, especially as the elite took a renewed interest in classical cultures. Art, science, and literature all contributed to geometric landscapes where social and artistic expression benefitted the educated. Probably the best-known example of a garden modeled on the Italian Renaissance is Versailles—André Le Notre's pleasure palace for the French aristocracy, where formal order dissolved into a distant wilder plane, hinting at a bridge between human and natural reason.

Our gardens today carry more than a hint of allegory, story, and privileged seclusion. Even our botanic gardens and national parks require entrance fees or great distances of travel to reach them, something many in our society can't afford. Gardens are places to visit, briefly experience, and then move on from. They are also places behind our homes and fences where we can't be disturbed, except by the errant neighbor's baseball or leaf blower. We go to nature, whether it's in a park or garden, to escape, to be cloistered, and to briefly be reminded of our shared lineage—even if that nature isn't wild but designed or accessed primarily for our own needs. We still keep nature at arm's length out of fear and disgust, as any weed treatment or pest spray commercial will demonstrate.

Perhaps no period in Western history has had as much influence on where our landscapes, and even our society, stand today as the Enlightenment, which occurred roughly from the late seventeenth to early nineteenth centuries. Philosophers such as John Locke and Jean-Jacques Rousseau transformed how we viewed and experienced nature, and these ideas would later manifest themselves in more extravagant Romanticism, which has also had a significant impact on our interactions with wildness.

Locke believed that all knowledge comes from sensory awareness of the world, that the human mind is the center of reason based on personal experience and reflection. As these ideas influenced garden and landscape design, landscapes became less about power, wealth, and social interaction and more about providing places for solitary reflection. Landscapes were paintings to induce a poetic feeling, and to spark personal thought that was more true than any social or cultural truth handed down by religion or politics. Gardens were places where an individual's wants, needs, and desires were paramount.

Rousseau saw such experiences as common across all peoples. To him, nature was a democratizer and equalizer because we all share in the same moment even as we do so apart from one another. Rousseau shifted landscape experience from purely artistic and literary to something more patriotic: landscapes to honor the common national experience, such as memorials for the dead, and eventually, the idea of public parks where all could enjoy the beauty of the countryside set apart from the cacophony of cities.

The Enlightenment's focus on rationalism—that humans can think logically through any issue and as a result be fulfilled and happier—in many ways ignored the other side of our being: raw emotion, which so often overtakes our ability to think or act clearly, but that we also need if we are to connect with the world. The nineteenth century brought about Romanticism, where landscapes became places for contemplation, meditation, reflection, and friendship—and above all intense sensory stimulation. Nature was seen more as a varied and diverse celebration than something to be reordered and interpreted, even while gardens practiced a careful rearrangement that sought to heighten the experience of a purer nature realized through the senses. It was English landscape gardener Lancelot "Capability" Brown who would spur the backlash against the intense color and form in Romantic gardens by making his landscapes rather plain, subtle, or picturesque. Brown's gardens embraced the space beyond their borders, working to make the immediate seem to go on toward the horizon. He saw the rural landscapes he loved as places where both work and pleasure could meld in harmony. Designing such spaces as the Hampton Court Palace gardens and areas around Highclere Castle (of Downton Abbey fame), he would often remove formal gardens in favor of hills, rivers, woodlands, and grasses—a different kind of order. Brown was known for moving massive amounts of soil to improve a landscape's contours, adding hedges to hide unsightly blemishes, and using a structure called the "ha-ha"—a fence hidden in a trench that kept livestock in their respective fields—to keep the long view unobstructed. Ultimately, Brown practiced a negotiation between wild nature and human rationalism, a subtle rural nature slightly elevated to tease mystery and emotion from shadows and curves.

It's Brown who in many ways gave us the idea of a garden as a wild, seemingly natural place, even as it is human made. Brown also influenced the famed American public park designer Frederick Law Olmsted. One of Olmsted's greatest concerns was free access to nature for people from all walks of life. He believed, in his own words, that "contemplation of natural scenes of an impressive character" heals us both physically and mentally and helps the mind be "occupied without purpose," easing the worries and stresses of life.

Central Park may be Olmsted's most revered landscape, but he also had much to do with preserving Yosemite, which served as a template for subsequent efforts like our first national park, Yellowstone. Established in 1864, Yosemite park was the first large expanse of wilderness set aside by Congress for the public. In the year following its opening, only a few hundred people visited; to do so, one had to hire a guide and horses, then travel 40 miles over uneven terrain. Olmsted predicted that within a century millions would visit every year (five million is the current average), and this would impact the stability of the landscape, especially the river. In tasking him to lead a commission on how to manage Yosemite, Congress empowered a new sense of engagement with scenic American sites. Careful to hide walking paths and roads behind tree lines and building integrated cabins and campsites, Olmsted set out to conceal the necessary infrastructure that would help Americans experience Yosemite's grandeur while attempting to preserve its wild character. To this day, the struggle to preserve Yosemite's beauty and ecology while allowing so many visitors to witness its power is still very real.

This level of landscape planning that combines human culture and wildness would be refined in two other Olmsted designs: the Biltmore Estate and the Fens and Riverway of Boston. At Biltmore, near Asheville in North Carolina, Olmsted was hired by industrialist George Vanderbilt to develop and improve nearly seven thousand acres of poor, over-farmed soils and forests that had been harvested of their most important trees. Olmsted strategically placed new fields and woodlands to take advantage of the site's natural conditions and put into place a management plan that would not be realized immediately but over decades. He believed that effective landscape design requires subsequent fine-tuning, often in the form of growth, succession, destruction, and thinning to benefit both human use and natural processes. In other words, to endure, majestic and ecologically meaningful landscapes require a long-term management plan.

During the late 1800s, Olmsted was also at work in Boston turning a floodplain polluted by sewage and industrial waste into a wetland that filtered water and prevented flooding. By developing both the infrastructure needed to move water and the planting schemes to treat it, Olmsted created an urban wilderness endemic to place. In 1883, he tasked Charles Sprague Sargent, director of Harvard University's Arnold Arboretum, to carefully select and place 100,000 native plants within a space that was a mere 2.5 acres. It was Olmsted's sincere hope that those who could not travel to the country to partake of wildness could at least experience some semblance of it within the city—and that such a semblance would not only be beautiful but also functional. Bucking the then-current trend of urban parks that were large, flat, formal, open green spaces, his landscapes would eventually be seen as entirely natural by subsequent generations, who assumed they had always existed in such a condition.

It is on this point that Anne Spirn, Professor of Landscape Architecture and Planning at MIT, reveals the double-edged success and failure of Olmsted. He succeeded in creating a human-made nature that allowed human and nonhuman cultures to intermingle, while taking into account the long-term management that would benefit both. But the landscape's artifice was so well concealed that the human element was lost, or these places were seen more as mere decoration rather than landscapes serving a literal purpose. Spirn goes on with her analysis:

> Landscapes blur the boundaries between the human and the nonhuman.... Calling some landscapes "natural" and others "artificial" or "cultural" ignores the fact that landscapes are never wholly one or the other. Such thinking promotes the persistent, common conception of the city as a degraded environment and wilderness as a pristine place untainted by human presence. Seeing humans, ourselves, as solely or mainly a contaminating influence prevents us from appreciating the potential beneficial effects we might have and limits what we can imagine as possible.

Of course, the first step to profound change and growth is awareness—in this case, awareness of our negative influences on nature. The next step is seeing our potential to be stewards of healthy landscapes in spite of our consumer-driven reality, integrating ourselves into the natural processes of the living systems that surround us. We aren't separate from nature but are deeply embedded in it. As such, we have the potential to evolve physically and emotionally with our landscapes. This sort of thinking drove such landscape design innovators as Jens Jensen, who, while traveling by rail across the Great Plains in the early 1900s, soulfully marveled at the vanishing prairie, then mimicked its form and function among the nature-deprived homes of Chicago's immigrant factory workers. Jensen sought a simultaneous awakening and conservation of nature that roused in people awe, empathy, and even daily appreciation of regional wildness.

Our greatest public landscape designers were surely influenced by Alexander von Humboldt, a Prussian geographer and world explorer. In the early nineteenth century, Humboldt began writing about nature in a new way—not out of fear or dread or alienation, as was a common trope, but with delight and fascination. Often referred to as the father of environmentalism, he would also influence the thinking of Henry David Thoreau and Charles Darwin, both of whom have shaped our trajectory in modern environmentalism and even garden making.

In this brief exploration of American naturalism, particularly as expressed through landscape design, it's helpful to note that in the United States our cultural traditions are less ingrained and less developed than those of Europe. In other words, landscape is not intimately part of our daily lives, but is seen as an existence outside of them. The separation of landscape and wildness from our culture both diminishes our love for nature while also romanticizing it as some lofty, almost untouchable experience to safely curate. Think about fossils at natural history museums, assortments of plants in gardens, or parks fenced in by parallel streets and buildings. Wild nature is truly another culture separate from our own.

And yet, American nature writers and visual artists often revere wildness, extolling its wholesome virtues. We still very much live in the time of Thoreau, John Muir, and others who idolize nature in an almost religious way, often seeing wilderness as the essence of our American character even as we become further and further removed from it. Maybe we're still trying to define nature, what role it has to play in shaping our beliefs and institutions, whereas in older cultures like those in Europe, culture and nature and landscape are more intertwined. Wildness in America is different though—in so many ways it's still among us, still this other we have to navigate, like settlers or conquistadors proving our mettle. There's a little bit of wild frontier left, and in many ways, seeing an end to that frontier will also mark an end to much of our cultural and social mythologies. So to take landscape design cues from European garden traditions may not always be appropriate, especially considering our still-functional wild places and wildlife. In other words, our native plants may play a more crucial philosophical and ecological role than in European landscapes, even as American garden designers look across the pond for inspiration.

Two of the most respected plantsmen, both in Europe and around the globe, are Noel Kingsbury and Piet Oudolf, proponents of the new perennial garden. Their work with and understanding of plant communities in garden design, often employing great numbers of native North American prairie plants left standing over winter, has led to a meaningful groundswell of change in how our urban landscapes look and an improvement in how well they function. These two men have collaborated on several publications that have been the impetus for new books that begin to Americanize certain principles—or begin to translate their revolutionary strategies for an American audience and ecology.

And while the artistic and sustainable practices these two have developed are making gardens more functional and even more wild, they have also decried the native plant perspective in America. Their viewpoint is not unique, so it serves as a good example to explore. In their book *Planting: A New Perspective*, Kingsbury and Oudolf reflect:

> The strictly nativist lobby, which believes in the exclusive use of regional natives, is not one which has arisen from within the garden and landscape communities, but rather has been imported from outside, from the world of environmentalist politics, where ecology is a word which can often weave dangerously between the evidence-based and scientific and the emotive and ideological. Unfortunately, the native plant lobby has on occasion acquired sufficient political support in some communities that the use of native plants has been mandated for landscaping projects, compromising their visual effectiveness and therefore the public support they receive.

It is unfortunate that environmental issues have become conflated with politics here, as so often happens when we need to dig deeper into the issues of our hand in nature. Are we uncomfortable digging deeper? Do we feel defensive? Why? For the landscape design profession to grow, and then by extension for private citizens to make sustainable choices based on examples they see, we need the garden conversation expanded and invigorated by diverse thoughts. Any practice which is not infused with ideas from other fields is lacking in its ability to adapt, evolve, and see beyond its relatively narrow field of vision.

Ultimately, every garden is an ideology. These ideologies are rooted in culture, class, and a plethora of other personal experiences and perspectives. If our gardens reflect an ideology that puts humans first, how is that a reflection of our other cultural beliefs and actions, from politely holding the door for someone to helping those in need? Insisting that a 100 percent native plant garden can't be stunning to the human eye is as myopic as insisting that the emotive and ideological can't be beneficial to garden making. Native plants are the tip of a much larger iceberg. The conversation goes well beyond what is native and why or how gardens work. The very fact that we keep having this conversation in publications, seminars, and podcasts, and that it makes some in horticulture uncomfortable, is evidence that we need to be having even larger conversations about why we garden and who we garden for, and what it means in a time of climate change and mass extinction. Our culture needs to be confronted in as many ways as possible for the sake of future human and nonhuman species.

In this spirit of exploring ecological value in our gardens, Kingsbury and Oudolf note the larger role our built landscapes play beyond aesthetic value:

> The food web which supports larger animals (mostly birds) is founded on invertebrates, chiefly insects. In many regions these are predominantly specialists—their larvae will *only* eat particular plants; a garden of introduced species will

therefore support very few of them and thus greatly impoverish the food web. However, most other animals are more generalist: nectar-drinking insects such as bees are not tied to native species in this way, and neither are berry-eating birds. Adding species to a locality through planting may actually improve the richness of the food web by providing nectar sources for bees at a time when the native flora has little to offer.

There's a lot that's troubling here, not the least of which is that the food web—whatever it is or however defined—mostly supports berry-eating birds (who do still feed insects to their young), when in fact there are a plethora of fauna interacting with our gardens above and below the soil line. Another issue revolves around the idea of generalist versus specialist species. In Chapter 2 we touched on how generalists need specialists and vice versa, and how in the case of native bees, the loss of specialists forced others to become specialists to the detriment of all bees and the plants being pollinated. Without the more nutritious pollen that bees need, their body weight and number of young diminish, jeopardizing the system or food web on even more complex levels. It's not the nectar that bees and many other insects need, it's the pollen—more specifically, the pollen they evolved with. Our gardens are complex ecosystems. It's incumbent upon us to see, value, and foster that complexity in every possible way as we honor wild relationships.

A final point by Kingsbury and Oudolf worth tackling is their argument about making wildness attractive to people, and especially on what plants to use:

> Planting design is, fundamentally, for people. In urban areas, planting in private gardens or public spaces is about providing a habitat for people. Anything which fails to interest or please them will lose support, as local governments that have created untidy "wildlife areas" in parks have found out to their cost. In regions where poisonous spiders and

snakes are common, there may be good reasons to actually fear such places! Areas for nature have to be seen to be attractive or in some way valued by people; only then will they gain political support. Using introduced species to provide interest for human users of landscape is one way to do this; very often non-gardening users of public spaces will find it easier to "read" a planting if some familiar cultivated plants are included.

Kingsbury, and certainly Oudolf, have made mainstream their ideas about how we can mesh habitat, low management, and beauty in landscape design. Terms like "drifts and masses," "plant communities," and "winter interest" have come to the forefront of landscape design so that spaces look and act more like their natural or wild origins, all while being accessible to us in the urban core. In so many ways, they've helped start us on a liberating journey that we're really just beginning to tap into via the new perennial movement. And so, thinking about the last quote above, I would assert that people do not need introduced plant species to find a space legible or welcoming or beautiful. A walk through any national park or refuge or prairie or wetland makes this reality evident.

It's brutally clear at this point in our planetary history that we need to rethink garden design. It cannot be solely or primarily for humans. We need places that provide habitat for people *and* other species so that we interact with wildness once again, realizing its value not just for ourselves but for itself. We need public landscapes that teach *and* welcome us in, through workshops, citizen science programs, benches, and interpretative signs. We need to stop fearing nature, keeping it at arm's length or in its proper place like a sculpture. Sometimes our landscapes will skew more toward other species as needed, and sometimes they will skew more toward the human. Regardless, our gardens must strive for a much more even playing field overall. And while we need wildness that is separate from us in parks and preserves—wildness even more free to pursue its own happiness—we also need designed wildness

in our everyday lives. If we expect to be selfless and compassionate toward one another, we first, or at least simultaneously, must
be selfless and compassionate to other species and to the greater-
than-human world.

As the monarch butterfly conservation initiatives sweeping our
nation now show, our interest in gardens goes far beyond how they
look. People are clamoring for landscapes to be more than being
pretty for us. They are hungry for meaning beyond what is currently offered. These calls for deeper substance should not be seen
as a threat to the garden design profession or horticulture industry,
but as an incredible opportunity to change our culture's perception
of wildness in the urban and suburban world, perhaps through
a far-reaching, big-hearted, activist-based ethics of compassion.
Even Emma Marris, a leader of the novel ecosystem movement,
insists: "While conservationists focus on 'pristine wilderness' only,
they give people the impression that that's all that nature is. And so
urban, suburban, and rural citizens believe that there is no nature
where they live; that it is far away and not their concern. They can
lose the ability to have spiritual and aesthetic experiences in more
humble natural settings." If, as Marris argues, nature and wildness
is our calling in the Anthropocene, how do we get wildness into
our daily lives?

It's difficult, whether we see it or not, to have the kinds of spiritual and aesthetic experiences that will reconnect us to nature. It's
difficult in a world of industrial agriculture that replaces wildness
and ecosystem function, as well as urban and suburban landscape
design—particularly when planting areas are simple afterthoughts
or last-minute decoration, as so often seems to be the case in most
built environments. It's difficult in a culture of "me" and "now." But
in order to create meaningful experiences for any length of time,
we have to choose plants that will perform the best in their intended locations and draw in and support the most wildlife.

In designing spaces that simultaneously foster meaningful experiences for humans and the means of survival for nonhumans,
we must consider various design aims. For instance, some people

might respond to butterflies and birds more than the arrangement of plants—or, maybe more precisely, the arrangement of plants could be the initial and momentary contact with a place, with nature, only one part of the significance of a place that lingers in us once we leave. Perhaps it's the arrangement of plants that draws us in, but it's arguably the wildlife those plants support that binds us to the spirit and purpose of the landscape. As a result, our gardens may need to practice a more overt ideology or activism beyond first-level beauty, all while opening us up to new sustainable and ethical possibilities.

Regardless of design strategy, native plants certainly tend to open us up to larger conversations that can be uncomfortable. Landscape architect Thomas Rainer, reflecting on the words of Piet Oudolf and Henk Gerritsen, further explores some of the above ideas:

> When it comes to plant selection, great plantsmen are often pragmatists, not crusaders. They are rarely ideological about where their plants come from or even how they are bred. At times they may favor wild plants, while at other times they prefer a cultivar. "We would rather have a vigorous monarda in our natural garden," write Piet Oudolf and Henk Gerritsen, "produced through a lengthy selection process (in other words, cultivated), than a wild specimen which degenerates into a pathetic pile of mildew in our climate." Sometimes the superior plant is a straight species. Other times it is a cultivar. What makes a garden-worthy plant is not the plant's pedigree, but its performance. This kind of ruthless meritocracy only allows the most vigorous, interesting, and worthy plants into a design.

What Rainer argues is absolutely logical. We have to make smart plant choices, ensuring our gardens perform well visually and as mutually supportive communities that require less human management. Making the right plant choices from an aesthetic and practical perspective is the first step in successful garden design.

The next crucial step though, I'd contend, is looking at each plant from the just-as-important perspective of faunal relationships. Often what this means is that we'll be choosing native plants to get the most bang for our buck, and that may mean not using those cultivars that can't support bees or butterflies. The ruthless meritocracy we need to be exercising doesn't stop at plant performance in a management or artistic sense, but extends equally beyond to the wildlife using the space over time.

As we aim to not only interpret wildness but also adapt it to our cities, we must consider plant origin and faunal interactions along with the established considerations of plant performance, suitability to site, and aesthetic appeal to humans. We also have to consider far more intensely how the plants will act with one another above and below the soil line. Tack on the need for phytoremediation—the use of plants to clean soil and water—and the new models for how to design and manage a garden require complex collaboration and thinking. We urgently need these new models. Our gardens can and should be doing far more than ornamenting our structures or punctuating the lunch hour, and we need to start teaching people about this new kind of gardening that the Earth so desperately requires. The best way to do that is to bring wildlife into people's visual field, and even into their laps—perhaps landing on their mealtime sandwiches and fruit cups—as often as possible throughout the day, every day. And the reasons why humans need more wildness are becoming well documented.

Students with views of nature out of the classroom window (not just a tree and some lawn, but real structured nature) show a 7 to 26 percent increase in test scores as well as enhanced creativity, critical thinking, ability to focus, and successful participation in group projects. Workers in office buildings with similar views have increased productivity and job satisfaction, while businesses save an estimated $93 million in annual healthcare costs. Hospital patients with even one tree out the window recover from illness and surgery faster. And for the economists among us, shoppers spend 115 to 125 percent more in a greener setting.

On a far more personal level, let me tell you about my grandmother. She lived in the highly compact and bustling suburb of Edina, Minnesota, two blocks from France Avenue, one of the busiest streets in the Twin Cities, flanked by shopping malls and restaurants. Next to her multistory condo building was a sidewalk that snaked around an artificial pond, with enough plantings of trees, shrubs, and flowers to make it aesthetically interesting. Workers from nearby office buildings ate snacks, talked on phones, or held mobile business meetings in the outdoor space, while families played on a minigolf putting green and drove remote-controlled boats on the water speckled with a few ducks. I think my grandmother's sanity was saved here, living alone, as she walked twice daily in this urban space lined with fledgling nature. And when Alzheimer's disease set in and she had to move to an assisted living facility, simply sitting on the front porch lined with a few potted geraniums and some maple trees along the street gave her a sense of peace, joy, and victory as she vanished into herself. The last time I ever spoke with her, she shared with me how thankful she was that she could still see a pond out back and the trees turning in autumn—and how these glimpses of nature reminded her of her daily walks at her previous home—walks that she believed she'd get to have again.

Yet I know these outdoor spaces could have been more meaningful and functional. The pond was treated with chemicals to keep it clean, the sides made of concrete and unable to touch plants or soil. When I walked with my grandmother, we heard birds but saw and experienced much less life than if the planting beds had been layered with plants to call in and support greater animal diversity. The assisted living building sported the standard landscaper fare of foundation bed and parking island plants, with street trees and accent trees to soften the structure's linear façade. This was no ecosystem that stretched beyond simple, efficient aesthetics, and I wonder what would happen for residents if more native wildness were present throughout the year. Would seeing a specific butterfly or moth laying eggs on a host plant awaken memories in an Alzheimer's patient like music has been shown to do, and for a moment build a bridge between who the disease has forced them to be and who they still are deep inside?

Nature heals. It bridges the gap. And when it gives life to other species and entire ecosystems, nature regains its inalienable purpose—especially in urban habitats. And while nature heals psychologically in profound ways, as it awakens and stirs biophilia and memory, it also heals in practical, measurable ways. Trees in city parks can remove 48 pounds of particulates, 9 pounds of nitrogen, 6 pounds of sulfur dioxide, and half a pound of carbon monoxide from the air each day. Dense trees like oak, hickory, and elm can lock up 10 to 40 tons of carbon per tree for centuries. Even our grasses and perennials get in on the act—Indiangrass and sunflowers remove toxic heavy metals such as mercury and lead, remediating soils contaminated by our industrial modern world.

A 2016 report from the Nature Conservancy entitled "Planting Healthy Air" explored 245 of the world's largest cities to see how or if urban tree planting would affect the health of residents neighborhood by neighborhood. With 70 percent of the world's population estimated to live in urban environments by 2050, the sustainability and health of those environments is critical. What the report shows is impressive: one tree can intercept 7 to 24 percent of particulate matter from the burning of fossil fuels within a 100-foot radius. Placing trees around those who are more susceptible to airborne pollution—including the young, elderly, and infirm—would have immediate health benefits. Think about the land that surrounds our schools, nursing homes, and hospitals. An annual $100 million global investment in strategic tree planting would help 68 million people and reduce air temperatures by 1 degree Celsius. Further, the report states that just four dollars spent per person could save eleven to thirty-six thousand lives annually. Some of the cities that could benefit most are in India and the

Middle East, but so could Louisville, Kentucky, a US city with one of the fastest-climbing heat island effects.

One mature street tree with a 30-foot crown can transpire 40 gallons of water a day, dropping surrounding temperatures by 2 to 9 degrees Fahrenheit—an important feature in cities where that heat island effect adds as much as 6 degrees during the day and 22 degrees at night. Tree-shaded surfaces—benches, walls, roofs—can be 20 to 45 degrees cooler in the summer, helping to reduce a structure's cooling needs anywhere from 7 to 47 percent. Green walls and green roofs also have measurable benefits, helping cool a surface by 10 degrees and reducing building energy use by 3 to 10 percent respectively.

The inverse is true, as well. Although the causes are multi-dimensional and complex, in spaces where nature is suffering, humans are manifesting the ill effects in the form of protests and riots. Climate change has been named a significant contributor to the Arab Spring of 2011 when civil unrest spread across the Middle East. Studies around the globe show how drought, floods, and higher temperatures are also spiking domestic violence, murder, and ethnic conflict. It's estimated that the predicted 2-degree Celsius rise of global temperature will mean a 50 percent increase in violence by 2040.

We can go even further, exploring how urban wild nature might help reduce crime. Two studies led by US Forest Service researchers looked at how certain land uses influenced criminal acts in Philadelphia, Baltimore, and Youngstown, Ohio. In 2000, Philadelphia launched a program to plant vegetation along roadways to absorb runoff. Researchers compared 52 of those newly vegetated plots with control plots that received no new greenery, tracking 14 types of crime in nearby areas. They found that narcotics possession in the greened areas dropped by 18 to 27 percent, even as the rate increased 65 percent citywide.

A similar effect occurred in eastern Ohio. From 2010 to 2014, Youngstown began converting vacant lots and rundown buildings into designed landscapes, even letting local communities turn them into parks, lawns, playgrounds, or gardens. The result was that areas of lawn maintained by contractors saw a drop in property crimes like theft, and community-maintained gardens saw violent crime drop precipitously.

It's not just heat or the addition of green spaces that can influence unrest, but also the pollution levels that permeate urban centers. By 2010 violent crime rates in cities like New York, Boston, Washington, Dallas, and Los Angeles fell by 58 to 78 percent from highs in the mid-1990s. One main theory links those earlier high crime rates to lead poisoning, specifically from the exhaust in cars and trucks. After lead was eliminated from gasoline in the 1970s, it still took more than twenty years for its effects to work through the population as it lingered in the environment. Even the tiniest amount of lead in our bodies leads to seismic increases in neurological damage. These minute levels reduce IQ through loss of neuron transmission in the brain, as well as a loss of gray matter in the prefrontal cortex—the area associated with aggression, impulse control, emotional regulation, attention, and verbal reasoning.

Of course, we live in a stew of human-spread chemicals on a grand scale, in such concoctions and numbers that we can barely begin to predict the long-term effects because most haven't been studied by the EPA. In the United States, 4 billion pounds of toxic chemicals—72 million of which are carcinogenic—are released into the atmosphere each year from twenty thousand industrial sites alone. Add two trillion pounds of livestock waste laced with antibiotics and hormones and our environment is radically changing. And it's often the poor or marginalized of our own species that are unfairly bearing the brunt of our toxic world. Eleven million Americans live within one mile of a federal Superfund site—a location contaminated with hazardous waste that poses a threat to human and environmental health. There are currently eighty thousand industrial chemicals in use globally, and more than seven hundred of those can be found in every human body. If our cities created spaces that were more reflective of how nature works—

with diverse structure and layers using trees, shrubs, grasses, and flowers that work in unison to clean our world—we'd be far healthier on untold levels, and would probably care more about the nature beyond the boundaries of our everyday lives.

How do we take back and detoxify our world using gardens and armed with our knowledge of plants? How do we encourage species to adapt and hold on as we figure out how to radically change our social and cultural models? How do we awaken to wildness that heals, restores, and binds us together? One promising way is through the evolution of public urban landscapes, as well as in our private gardens.

For practical steps to remake our gardens, we can look to Travis Beck, landscape architect and director of horticulture at the Mt. Cuba Center in Delaware:

> For long term stability in the face of environmental fluctuations, broad-scale resistance to pests and pathogens, and the ability to continue to evolve, genetic diversity in a plant population is essential. This is as true in the constructed landscape as it is in nature. To benefit from these advantages of intraspecific diversity, designers should use cultivated varieties selectively, consider developing regional or site-specific landraces, and insist on broad-based collection of seed for the production of straight species for landscape use.

Beck's proposals would help ensure the health and function of our urban landscapes, while encouraging plants and wildlife to adapt to the concrete jungle. By using native plant species, especially those of local genetic origin, we could give our landscapes a leg up on adaptation to bring wildness into our lives, bridging the many natures of our existence. Plants would not be just pretty—they would also be useful as they clean the environment, preserve precious topsoil, increase our mental health, decrease our dependence on fossil fuels, and sustain wildlife via multiple functions.

In a ten-part series featured on the American Society of Landscape Architects' blog *The Field*, David Hopman, associate professor at the University of Texas at Arlington and research associate
at the Botanical Research Institute of Texas, explores the ways in
which our landscapes must change, with inspiring examples and
success stories leading the charge. Early in his series, he explores
how aesthetics, environment, and ecology intersect in landscape
design, and how privileging one over the other has dire effects on
what we hope to achieve. Specifically, Hopman defines the three
core areas of design as follows: 1) Aesthetics—for the enhance-
ment and intensification of everyday use, and characterized by
balance, texture, scale, color theory, line, et cetera, as well as psychology, cultural influence, and social expectations; 2) Environment—making use of phytoremediation, carbon sequestration,
reducing human inputs, and the like; and 3) Ecology—he uses the
Cary Institute's definition: "The scientific study of the processes
influencing the distribution and abundance of organisms, the interaction among organisms, and the transformation and flux of
energy and matter." Hopman is critical of some botanic gardens
because they give everyday folks a false sense of success in landscapes that don't balance the three core areas of solid design. The
imbalance is particularly noticeable when those landscapes focus
almost solely on aesthetics, in effect becoming art museums for
plants—especially when such landscapes don't advertise themselves as exactly what they are.

There are several roadblocks, Hopman notes, to creating landscapes that successfully balance aesthetics, environment, and ecology. One of them is a horticulture industry that generally, though
not always, continues to produce exotic invasives, promotes monocultures through simplistic plant choices, and limits native plant
inventory (especially among the largest growers). There's still room
for significant improvements on all these fronts, particularly for an
industry centered on utility that's not region specific and a landscape design industry that relies too much on masses of the same
plant rather than plants intermingling as they do in nature. There's

also a continued reliance on and preference for wood mulch as a key design element when green mulch—plants—is what's needed to ensure a functional living system. A major challenge is creating effective examples on large scales that the public can experience, learn from, and emulate at home with some modicum of success.

Several recently completed success stories showcase sustainable and more naturally wild urban landscapes. Though all of these are big-budget projects with costs in the millions and tens of millions of dollars, the important takeaway is that they are private/public partnerships that spread the cost between multiple groups and create a new level of civic engagement, while inspiring visitors with a profound design aesthetic. More critically, they focus on environmental and ecological sustainability, often using a significant number of plants native to the area as well as wilder spaces left to evolve. Most of these urban landscapes also incorporate multiple levels of education and outreach, serving as community hubs. When our landscapes become desirable public places for the exchange of experiences, human to human and animal to human, our communities reap substantial benefits.

Let's briefly look at three landscapes in medium to large urban centers to explore the shifting tide of sustainable and ethical landscape design. The first is in Dallas on the eastern edge of the campus of Southern Methodist University: the George W. Bush Presidential Center, completed in 2013. This 24-acre site holds a 15-acre public park that's a visual and environmental marvel. Designed by Michael Van Valkenburgh Associates, the entire landscape treats more than 90 percent of its annual rainfall and removes 85 percent of solids in the runoff from hard surfaces. The system of limestone seeps and bioswales leads to a wet prairie that recharges a 250,000-gallon cistern, which reduces annual irrigation by 73 percent or 6.1 million gallons a year. In addition, the lawn and hellstrips are composed of a mix of native shortgrasses and require only four annual mowings, saving $41,000 every year.

The one-mile trail system is modest but takes visitors through rolling hills, open areas, and dry water features that highlight native ecoregions in the area—from blackland prairie to post oak savannah to cross timbers forest composed of oak, hickory, ash, and cedar. Every portion of the landscape uses organic methods to build the soil and food web over time, and hand weeding is the primary means of control, especially in areas that are early in their establishment. It is a thick, lush, dynamic garden that looks good in winter and brings nature right up to those who visit. Dallas is also in the planning stages of an even larger park, one of the largest in the nation, what they are calling a nature district. At 10,000 acres, it will hug the Trinity River and be composed of wetlands, forests, trails, and open greenspaces.

A second notable landscape is Mill River Park in Stamford, Connecticut, a 14-acre greenway along the Mill River, also known as the Rippowam River, as named by native Algonquins. This stretch of waterway had become severely polluted, full of debris and silt. Concrete dams that were intended to mitigate floods had actually increased their intensity. The dams were removed and the river bed dredged and reworked, creating riffles, pools, and meanders that mimic the waterway's natural form and function. This work led to river herring returning to spawn for the first time in 360 years.

Mill River Park is visually impressive—so much so that you'd almost assume it wasn't made by humans. The banks are covered in layers of native vegetation from flowers to shrubs and trees, and anyone can walk right up to the water's edge or venture out atop boulders. Designed by the Olin Studio in partnership with the Army Corps of Engineers and a team of ecologists, the park's purpose is not only ecological but social sustainability. The nonprofit Mill River Park Collaborative oversees all levels of maintenance, operation, and public programming by contract with the city. Some of the main programs include creating outdoor classrooms for elementary science teachers and employing paid high-school interns who learn about land management, run a native plant nursery, and perform outreach in the community. The internship program is particularly innovative, giving students from all walks of life not only cold hard cash but valuable career training and guidance in environmental fields.

Operating on a much larger scale than either the Bush Center or Mill River Park is a third landscape of note. Forest Park in St. Louis, Missouri, is a 1,370-acre urban park opened in 1876 that hosted both the 1904 Summer Olympics and the 1904 World's Fair. The park is home to a diversity of institutions, including the St. Louis Zoo, Art Museum, Science Center, and the Missouri History Museum—not to mention golf courses and other recreational sports fields. In the early 2000s, large portions of it began intensive modernization and natural restoration with the help of Oehme, van Sweden & Associates. These restorations include prairies and wetlands that will reduce maintenance costs and increase wildlife use. In total, 170 acres of the landscape are considered wild and are laid out to create wildlife corridors composed of over 1,200 recorded plant, bird, and insect species. In fact, the entire park is an important waystation for birds migrating along the Mississippi Flyway in spring and fall.

Several large areas bring wildness and ecosystem function into the heart of this large urban park. The 60-acre John F. Kennedy Memorial Forest in the southwest corner is the oldest conservation area and contains an 8-acre savanna reseeded by volunteers beginning in 1999. Additional natural landscapes include the 24-acre Deer Lake Savanna, the smaller Hidden Creek Savanna restored by Missouri Master Naturalists, and the 20-acre Successional Forest. The last area has been left to its own devices for thirty years and is evolving from a mowed expanse with landscape trees into a multilayered ecosystem.

My own city, Lincoln, Nebraska, is in the planning stages of the $13-million Haines Branch Prairie Corridor, which will link two prairie remnants and a park on the west side of town with a large citywide trail network. The nearly 20-mile round-trip will pass through 7,400 acres; 3,400 acres of that area is currently tallgrass prairie, and an additional 2,000 acres will be established as tallgrass. Add in a diversity of wetland and riparian areas, including

30 acres of critically endangered saline wetlands, and Lincoln may be positioned to become the prairie capital of the state.

What all of the above urban landscapes do is open the way for new ideas of garden design. While each is a distinct park focused on human use, holding traditional functions from concerts to sports to biking, they also bring wildness closer to human culture. Certainly, some examples like the Bush Center and Mill River Park look almost entirely wild, but they are also very intentional spaces designed with knowledge spanning architecture, ecology, and civics. In other words, they more successfully negotiate the human and the nonhuman worlds, and help us reconceptualize what urban spaces can look and feel like. Other, more intensively designed spaces—including the High Line in New York City— help bridge the garden/wild divide in a clear departure from traditional landscape design (especially commercial "landscaping") that uses unsuitable plants in non-functioning and unnatural arrangements.

Changing our cultural expectations and assumptions about landscapes may come down to blending our imposed sense of order with the perceived sense of disorder in nature—that very same disorder that we flock to admire on vacations, that physically and mentally heals us, but that we also believe threatens us at home and school because it might harbor "pests" like snakes, mice, and bees.

One of the earliest and most important pieces on designing wildlife gardens that win over the public is Joan Iverson Nassauer's "Messy Ecosystems, Orderly Frames." Nassauer says that ecological function is not readily recognizable to anyone but those trained to know, so special "cues to care" must be used to help humans interact with the design. While it's too bad that we can't just let nature perform its self-ordering in urban and suburban areas, we must embrace our cultural lenses. How do we do that? Maybe we place new, unrecognizable plants that perform desirable ecosystem services among others the public already knows and can connect with, like purple coneflowers or coreopsis. We can do that on a large scale by having a "wilder" meadow or prairie augmented by lawn, dotted with benches or tables or arbors or swing sets, and even (if we must) a sweep of hybrid roses. In the end, Nassauer contends: "While a neat landscape is the unmistakable product of human intention, a natural looking landscape is more likely to be misinterpreted. Nature is a cultural concept that is frequently mistaken as an indication of ecological quality. It has no specific appearance in form and may be as readily applied to a canopied urban plaza or a cultivated field." Our task at hand is to make natural patterns legible while not losing the wildness of those patterns. In other words, we not only have to bring functional nature home, we have to change how we see nature—both as a pretty vista and as a function of physical and psychological health. Where we may find nature working can be almost anywhere, and to what degree it's working says a lot about our belief in what nature is and what role it has to play in our daily lives.

The world is changing for the better. The 2016 hot trends that residential consumers are demanding from landscapers and nurseries are native plants, drought-tolerant landscapes, and sustainable design that helps wildlife—and it mirrors the same list from the year before:

ASLA 2016 Residential Landscape Architecture Trends
+ 88% rainwater/graywater harvesting
+ 86% native plants
+ 85% native/adapted drought-tolerant plants
+ 85% low maintenance
+ 77% permeable paving
+ 75% foodscapes
+ 73% rain gardens
+ 72% lawn reduction

This same year, the Landscape Architecture Foundation (LAF) released their New Landscape Declaration for the next 50 years; in it, they call for landscape architects to advocate for a significant change in sustainable design, similar to how scientists are currently calling upon one another to be activists regarding climate change. The wordage the LAF agreed on in the declaration is exciting:

> What we do to our landscapes we ultimately do to ourselves. The profession charged with designing this common ground is landscape architecture.... After centuries of mistakenly believing we could exploit nature without consequence, we have now entered an age of extreme climate change marked by rising seas, resource depletion, desertification and unprecedented rates of species extinction. Set against the global phenomenon of accelerating consumption, urbanization and inequity, these influences disproportionately affect the poor and will impact everyone, everywhere. The urgent challenge before us is to redesign our communities in the context of their bioregional landscapes enabling them to adapt to climate change and mitigate its root causes.

In response to both the ASLA list and LAF declaration, I feel simultaneous loss and excitement. As a prairie hugger, I'm impatient as I watch landscapes and species vanish under a multipronged onslaught in one of the most threatened ecosystems on the globe. Too often change must come slowly, filtered and trickled down through imposing bureaucracy and politics, ideologies rooted in conserving the status quo, all the while ensuring that those in power maintain their influence. This glacial process is when we're told by the system to meet people in the middle, or that baby steps are the best and only way to garner positive adoption. I can't help but feel we need multiple approaches with multiple perspectives, that we need to feel more uncomfortable and thus less complacent. No effective social change has ever been universally or quickly accepted, but much has wiggled its way into our daily lives after explosive beginnings and even explosive recurrences after the changes weren't made. And when a social change also asks us to look at our culture through the eyes of other cultures, to perceive society as more than human or more than singular, change becomes doubly challenging.

I'm calling for our personal landscapes to be explosive so that, sooner rather than later, a new garden design ethic gains traction in the suburban and urban world. If the ship is going down—if we're causing 60 percent species loss this century and are committed to a global temperature rise that displaces billions of people while exacerbating violence—then there's no reason not to scream and act with extreme empathy as the ship slips beneath the rising waves. No theory of novel ecosystems, helping us assuage our guilt and spin the potential outcome to a veneer of happiness, will change the fact that we need plants—native plants, in radically new landscapes—and that all life needs native plant gardens at every scale to have a fighting chance. Do not give up on wildness, even in the Anthropocene. The wild still dwells among us, hoping for a revival of our compassion.

I'm constantly on the lookout for native plant gardens, or beds of even the smallest size, in public areas of my city. It's not that easy, especially locating ones that are multileveled, look pleasing to the human eye, and function ecologically year round. One summer I attempted to document every public native plant bed in town, no matter its size or status. Someone told me about a few hellstrips downtown near a hotel, narrow beds that occupied the daunting expanse between street and sidewalk. On a weekend afternoon, I did a drive-by, and then another drive-by because I missed them the first time around.

Getting out of the car with the Sun to my back as evening approached, I saw that late summer and early fall asters were in bloom, while grasses arched over just beyond the confines of their rectangular oasis careful not to trip or touch any pedestrian. I took pictures from every angle as a man and his dog walked by pretending not to notice. I cautiously put my left leg out into the street while occasional drivers made the turn headed toward a residential area; otherwise the only thing I could hear was a delivery truck bouncing in the distance. As I walked north, I was taken aback at what I saw—an awkwardly tall *Liatris ligulistylis* that stood out from its barren bed like a pre-teen with an early growth spurt.

The blooms were almost fluorescent violet, gaudy against the red façade of the hotel and the silver concrete that covered the ground plane. By itself, meadow blazingstar looks like a very pretty weed. Some even mistake it for a thistle. The quarter-inch flowers are far apart, blooming from the top down, and the leaves are thin and narrow like pine needles. Alone like this, it really wasn't a pretty sight, but it was a start. Surrounded by washed-out mulch, I'm not sure how it had survived, especially near the corner where it must receive all kinds of grit and debris. But it wasn't just the marvel of this northern prairie native thriving in harsh conditions; it was the monarch butterfly leaping up and down the stem to nectar on its second-favorite plant. That bright orange bouncing in a calculated ricochet from flower to flower provided a fourth dimension—one that went beyond the plant itself and out into time and space. Surprisingly, no one slammed on their brakes to leap out and admire the scene with me. The woman standing at the crosswalk with a shopping bag made her way the instant the light turned. I wondered if the occasional people around me would wake the next morning to a news headline that read, "Killed by motorist, man observing city butterfly was searching for urban wildness." If I'd located it, I wasn't sure, but the monarch and I briefly found one another in the fading prairie light of August.

Speaking the Language Again

Maybe native intelligence of a different
kind than human is just as intelligent
as our own but without the monuments
erected by it. Maybe intelligence isn't
simply writing or building structures.

—LOREN EISELEY

T HERE'S FROST on the garden this morning. The young
meadow I seeded in the lawn is speckled in off-white, the
bumps of bunchgrasses highlighted by deep folds of shadows
where the frost could not hold. I quickly walk this small landscape,
penetrating the chill of early morning, the cloak of a warm shower
shielding me from the sting. But I yearn for that sting, too, so I
walk barefoot over the crystals and fallen leaves, every step loud
and disruptive. There's something about the scent of an autumn
morning like this one—sunlight cresting the neighbor's hill, rays of
warmth making seeds of aster and goldenrod drip with dampness.
What is that scent? It's almost imperceptible—the tanned leather
of a jacket, the coffee in a long-forgotten mug, the slight pause
after a rainfall when nothing moves in the sweetened air.

I take for granted my walks, steps many others are unable to take. Knees give out, hearts weaken, there are jobs and children and parents to look after. It's such a short time that the frost endures in morning light, and even in the red cedar shadows, it can't hold on long. I remember walking the wheat field where my family settled on an Oklahoma prairie 120 years ago. Each step through last year's stubble was like thunder, the sound of seed heads against my jeans a washboard's echo. Kneeling on that soil, head hardly above the new crop, the future and the past were suddenly focused like a vise on my presence in that one moment. I heard the last two standing walls of the barn move in the breeze, nails sliding in and out of emaciated boards. I tasted the chaff of harvest on a hot June evening when I was nine, chasing down the dust in my throat with sweet iced tea. And then, a moment later, I'm in Minnesota tracing my hands over pine needles on the ground, fitting the tips of my small fingers into cones lying atop them like some wreckage washed ashore. And then I'm a husband in Nebraska, my fingernails black with earth, my skin broken and bleeding, my back burned and peeling, some feigned image of what the world should or could look like grazing the edges of my fenced-in reality. What is a garden? Who is it for? Why does it matter? Can and should it matter beyond this small space and this one moment?

A garden is a field of row crops. A garden is an expanse of lawn. A garden is a line of well-spaced hosta plants in a swath of wood mulch. A garden is a tree between the sidewalk and the street. A garden is a potted geranium. A garden is a prairie burning in the springtime. A garden is a fishery, a coal mine, a nuclear reactor— they all affect a functioning planet. And so a garden is a mythology of culture, class, economy, belief, and subjectively lived experiences. A garden is an ideology as sure as voting or painting or writing or loving. Our world, the intimate one of our daily lives and the more abstract one beyond our immediate reach, is alive with senescence as it decays and rebuilds itself. Every day we take away and add to life with each act or thought, our languages filled with communicating emotions we've barely formed inside before we let them loose. A garden is a place to learn from the voices of others.

Earth is filled with languages of all kinds that humble, awaken, and connect us. When we start to learn those languages, we may begin to see through the eyes of those that speak another tongue while fighting for the landscapes we all need together. Treehoppers, for example, use their thorax muscles to shake their abdomen, which vibrates through stems so other treehoppers within a meter can detect them. Crickets rub their tuning-fork legs at so many pulses per second, the number geared toward likely mates of the same species. Flowers change color to notify pollinators when the nectar runs out, as well as producing an electrical charge that lets bees know when and when not to visit a bloom. Those same flowers have petals lined in ultraviolet runways to guide insects toward pollen and nectar. The sticky glue on spider webs has electrostatic properties that make it lurch out toward prey, distorting the Earth's electric field within a few millimeters. Spider webs also collect small airborne particles, actively filtering pollutants with an efficiency equal to the best industrial scrubbers in smokestacks.

We are connected to life through knowledge, whether it's scientific or perceptual. We are made of exploded stars. We are affected by the stuff we cultivate. The soil bacteria *Mycobacterium vaccae* may activate neurons in the brain that contain serotonin, the chemical whose lack may cause depression. Even the blood of plants is the blood of humans—the only significant difference is the magnesium atom in chlorophyll and the iron atom in hemoglobin. One captures light, the other oxygen.

There is an intelligence beyond ours, and when we begin to comprehend it—even without deciphering it—we're better able to gain empathy if not compassion for others. Perhaps it's not an intelligence beyond us, not really, but a way of being that confounds our complexity of emotion and culture, those made-up distortions of shared and lived experience that aren't so different yet tend to make us feel separated.

Even plants share many of our hardwired traits to survive and function well. There's a weed in the mustard family, *Arabidopsis thaliana*, that performs math to stay alive. Scientists at the UK's John Innes Centre explored the starch the plants make by photosynthesizing sunlight. At night the plants take stock of how much starch is left in their leaves, guess how long it is until dawn, then portion out the starch. These plants are so accurate, they consume about 95 percent of their starch by sunrise—no waste, no deficit.

Other plants can recognize their kin, like the sea rocket. If it detects an unrelated plant, it will aggressively send out roots to stake its claim to soil nutrients, but if the other plant is a relative, it will restrain itself from growing too much or too fast. There are even plants that sense neighbors by minute changes in light. All plants absorb and reflect different wavelengths; some can detect when humans are near them or farther away, and even what color our clothing is, by using photoreceptors to process the reflected light.

Plants may also have a rudimentary nervous system similar to animals. The proof comes from Ted Farmer at the University of Lausanne who placed microelectrodes on the leaves and stalks of *Arabidopsis*, or rock cress, the floral equivalent of a lab rat. Farmer's team wanted to see how plants transmit information while under attack, specifically looking at electrical signals. After allowing Egyptian cotton leafworms to feast on the plant, it only took a few seconds of damage for voltage changes in the leaf tissue to radiate out to undamaged areas of the plant. As those signals moved through the tissue, the plant produced a defensive compound called jasmonic acid. Even more interesting, the genes that transmit the signal also produce channels along the plant's cell walls that help regulate ions that pass on the information. The result? Massive similarities to the animal, and human, nervous systems.

Almost every plant observed that defends itself from predators will also release volatile organic compounds, or VOCs; the sweet smell of cut grass is an example. Some studies show that when lima beans are exposed to VOCs of other lima beans, they grow faster to resist attack by insect pests. The same response occurs with corn seedlings so they can, as they get older, fend off beet armyworms. VOCs from sagebrush elicit defensive responses in tobacco, and chili peppers react to cucumber emissions.

Plants not only talk to each other, but can also communicate with other life forms—for example, by sending out an SOS to insect predators. Maize assaulted by beet armyworms attracts wasps that lay eggs on the armyworm's larvae. What else gets called in to fight in this war of the worlds? Ants, soil microbes, hummingbirds, even tortoises—they all react to VOCs.

Plants communicate via soil to let one another know of impending drought conditions, often prompting them to close their stomata so water doesn't escape their leaves.[1] And it's not just stressed plants that communicate but also unstressed plants who pass along knowledge. Scientists hypothesize that plants like peas and some wildflowers forward information via chemicals released into the ground. One study explored clicking sounds made by some young plants grown in water; when sounds in the same frequency range as that clicking were played back to the roots, the roots bent toward the sound. Is this another method of surviving drought? And the potentially unnerving thought is, will we genetically engineer plants that click to one another, smell to one another, all for the sake of better yields or prettier looks? Worse still, what happens when we create plants that can't talk to one another, that lose their language and in essence have their culture decimated? What would be the repercussions of such changes on ecology and biodiversity, on ecosystems both novel and remnant?

There's so much to this world we know barely anything about, let alone understand—call it a wisdom much older than ours, or call it another culture. As we learn more and more about life, we can learn more and more about our own lives and societies that will lead to profound scientific and ethical breakthroughs. In an 1880 article, Charles Darwin and his son Francis shared experiments showing that the growing tip of plants can essentially see light, and thus guide growth toward the Sun. Of course, we've since learned how to use light to cultivate plants. During World War II, scientists discovered how to manipulate the flowering process by turning lights on and off. They kept soybeans from blooming by turning lights on for only a few minutes each night, and conversely, made irises bloom in the middle of winter. This research shows plants don't measure length of day but rather periods of darkness, paving the way for growers to time flowers for Mother's Day sales.

While plants seek the color blue as they grow toward sunlight, it's red light that tricks them into blooming. And there are different kinds of red light, such as far red, which has longer wavelengths that occur at dusk, whereas pure red light occurs at dawn. Shine red light on irises to make them bloom, then a moment of far red light and they won't bloom; but shine them with red again, and they will bloom after all.

There's even more light to shed on plants. Blue light is a beacon of sorts that plants reach toward, but it also defines a circadian rhythm or clock that regulates leaf movements toward the Sun, as well as the process of photosynthesis. We humans have a circadian clock also, and it can be reset by sunlight, which is why jet lag is best treated by being outdoors. Plants and animals aren't the only ones to have an internal clock—bacteria and fungi do, too.

You can see what this series of examples is building toward. Plants exhibit senses similar to our own. There is an awareness, a language, even a rudimentary intelligence at work in their bodies. We know plants also respond to touch; sensitive ferns are an obvious example, but so are vines that reach out to feel for an object they can twine around. Trees know when they're swaying in the wind. Mustard plants stroked three times a day are shorter and flower later than those left unmolested; even more surprising, the genetic makeup of those touched plants changes. Similarly, a species of tree might produce individuals that are tall and fully branched in a calm valley, but short and thick on a windy hilltop.

Genes in plants are turned on and off to adapt to the conditions they find themselves in. Humans do this, too: trauma, either physical or emotional, can be passed on genetically to the next generation, affecting how we think, react, and participate in the world around us.

When we come to know the language of other species—whether we understand the syntax or not, whether we can communicate with it or not—we come to know the full power of this language and how it touches the entire landscape. When we see other species whose lives don't need our hand in their own, species who in fact thrive despite or in spite of us, we come to a more powerful center of strength inside of ourselves. So often our language takes us away from ourselves and even further from the world—stilted jargons of law and commerce, languages of superiority and separation.[2] But when our language is one of community, equality, patient understanding, of displacing ourselves for even a moment in the face of another's experience or intelligence, we come into a fuller compassion that stretches our existence.

In his book *Last Child in the Woods*, Richard Louv speaks to how we teach our kids lessons that alienate them from life. When we say rainforests are vanishing or you must recycle to save the planet, we disassociate children from life. Louv suggests that "in our zest for making them aware of and responsible for the world's problems, we cut our children off from their roots." Instead of presenting nature as a place of joy and wonder and discovery, we paint a picture of nature on life support in the end times. Louv goes on to say how kids (and even adults) cut themselves off from painful emotion as a self-preservation mechanism, particularly after trauma like physical abuse, and the same kind of self preservation might be happening with our talk on climate change and extinction.

If, as Louv suggests, we are practicing self-preservation by cutting ourselves off from nature, and by extension the trauma we cause the environment, then why do we have parks? Why do we have zoos? Why do we have gardens? Why are rents on apartments with a view of Central Park exponentially higher than those without? Why do we have stuffed animals? As we displace animals in zoos and plants in gardens, often cutting them off from their wild meaning, we become more displaced among our world and know it, if only subconsciously. And yet we are still seeking a language to bridge the gap between ourselves and wildness—but only within the context of our perception, our needs, and our desires. Derrick Jensen reflects, "There is a language older by far and deeper than words. It is the language of bodies, of body on body, wind on snow, rain on trees, wave on stone. It is a language of dreams, of gesture, of symbol, of memory. We have forgotten this language, forgotten it for so long we do not even remember that it exists. If we are to survive, we must again remember this language. We must learn how to think like the planet."

In our history we've even created languages around flowers, hoping metaphor and symbol would convey what our culture wouldn't allow us or we wouldn't allow ourselves to say. The art of ikebana, Japanese flower arranging, began as a way for women to silently communicate with stern samurai husbands; spoken words would have been an intrusion and presumption on the part of wives. Similarly, illiterate Ottoman women, wives and mistresses confined to their living quarters, devised a language using flowers to subvert their forced illiteracy.

Likewise, in Victorian England, floriography was developed to express emotions and desires considered outwardly taboo in a socially conservative culture. Women and men alike consulted dictionaries that translated the meaning of a bouquet delivered to them, all the way down to individual flowers and stems from various plants. Perhaps an arrangement would spell out sexual longing and a clandestine meeting behind the waxworks, or sadness and doubt for a relationship on the rocks. Today we give flowers primarily on marked occasions with obvious cookie-cutter messages. Flowers are a careful message of nature brought indoors, sterilized, perfected for a moment—choked off reminders that the world talks to us only in whatever our perception of beauty might be.

We find language in other ways as well, trying to understand the communications going on around us, perhaps as a way to belong or find our way through life. Mathematics has revealed the fractal backbone of nature; so many elements in our landscapes are equations that can be mapped out and predicted as they are given form. Fractals can be entire galaxies, clouds, mountain ranges, coastlines, forests, and sunflowers. They can also be nervous and circulatory systems, the movement of our eyes, cancer cells, and our heartbeats. If we can map our heart's rhythms, we might be able to identify risk for heart attacks long before they occur. We can use fractal algorithms to predict if blood vessels will form cancer cells. Entire forests could be mapped by studying just a few trees, helping us predict the ecosystem's impact on the environment, such as its carbon sequestration over time. Fractals have even given us cell phone communication that allows simultaneous phone calls, texting, and internet browsing.

In a sense, our effort to communicate with one another—especially in the context of our natural world—has created entire subcultures. As we perceive seeming chaos around us in the form of lost jobs, lost love, disease, and bad weather, we still look for an underlying order, going so far as to create it ourselves however possible. In the creation of a subculture, like floriography or garden making for wildlife, we are responding to ideals—hopes and fears, victories and sorrows. In a way, our myriad languages—whether scientific, psychological, or even religious—are working to bridge the gaps our evolved minds have created between nature and ourselves, between who we imagine our best selves to be and who we understand our worst selves to be.

Author Scott Russell Sanders observes:

> The root meaning of religion is to bind together. The only way to avoid being religious in that original sense, is to pretend that the universe does not cohere. It does cohere,

beautifully. On every scale we have been able to examine, from quarks to supergalactic clusters, we find structure. Even what we used to label chaos now appears to obey rules. In the history of science, every time we have come up against phenomena that seemed haphazard, they turned out to be lawful on a scale we had not yet grasped.

If we take the root meaning of religion to mean a binding together, then in a powerful way, every action we take to understand life—to communicate our emotions—is a spiritual act of profound coherence. Even if such coherence is imperfect, or formed in the forge of oppression or loss or fear, we are seeking a language that knows all life. There's a reason so many of the Earth's populations are religious, following an institutional belief system that subscribes to a set of ethical laws. We are constantly seeking coherence.

What if we saw holy texts as philosophical texts, as pieces of literature, as our languages and our cultures reaching out to other species and wild spaces to find our place in life? Every major religious text holds vast nuggets of environmental and even ecological awareness—instructions on how to respectfully treat the world. Of course, interpretations of the Bible and Quran, like interpretations of law or emotion, can be highly subjective and used by those in power to meet their own nefarious ends. But by looking at just a small sample, it's easy to see how the basis of religion is an act of binding together humanity and creation, spiritual and physical. Perhaps gardens in their best sense act like this, too.

Wendell Berry asserts that biblical passages experienced indoors seem improbable or fanciful, but when read outdoors become natural and full of wonder. He proposes, "Whoever really has considered the lilies of the field or the birds of the air and pondered the improbability of their existence in this warm world within the cold and empty stellar distances will hardly balk at the turning of water into wine—which was, after all, a very small miracle. We forget the greater and still continuing miracle by which water (with soil and sunlight) is turned into grapes."

Can one argue that the Bible is a green book, especially in the context that Berry places it in our daily lives awash in nature? Absolutely. In its distilled form, it's a manifesto for respecting, healing, and cultivating life in the spirit of its wild existence. In his essay "Christianity as Ecologically Responsible," David Kinsley says the Bible shows how nature is alive and animate, part of the holy conversation between god and life on Earth, especially between god and human consciousness. At the core, restraint on dominion is the message, with passages that restrict tree cutting and admonishments to leave the land fallow to heal, and to steward animals with compassion. And then there's Proverbs 31:8, which states, "Speak up for those who cannot speak for themselves, for the rights of all who are destitute." How can one not think of plants and animals who are left without food and shelter as we erode their ecosystems?

Generations of thinkers who have followed in the biblical tradition show the text's language as healing and understanding nature, not deposing it. St. Augustine perceived god as diffused through all of nature, as artist and shepherd, and this careful existence is instructive on how we should act in the world. There's also Francis of Assisi, who saw all creatures not as something other but as brothers and sisters, and who was purported to communicate with them. Saint Francis praised all aspects of the world—from animals to mountains and rivers to fire and wind—as being part of a divine consciousness that bound life together in equality and mutual understanding. Such a perspective is rare in Western culture but prevalent in other cultural traditions, especially those of east Asia, like Buddhism.

Perhaps Islam and the Quran take religious greening further than the Bible, if not more explicitly so, even as there are many parallels. For example, the environment is god's creation and to preserve it signals divine respect; while the Earth exists for human use, it is not exclusively or even primarily so. In fact, every entity on Earth is in continuous praise of the creator, and while humans may not understand the language others use to express their praise, this is reason enough not to diminish that praise by eradicating a species or a place. And while the universe's balance was created by god, and humans are at the top of the hierarchy, creation is not just for the present generation of life; humans have been entrusted to maintain environmental balance, even if it means planting a palm shoot the day before the end of the world. Additionally, Persian and later Islamic gardens are seen as previews of a paradise or afterlife, in that they help us see beyond the human to the spiritual, and so are an act of gratitude for this life and the next.

We can and maybe should look to religious texts like the Bible and the Quran for environmental guidance, especially as we address our emotional divorce from nature through violence, greed, and a fear of the living world. Given that so much of the world's population ascribes daily to the fundamental tenets of one religion or another, or lives within cultures based on some meaningful aspect of religion and spirituality, it's paramount that we rethink theology not as an oppressor but as a liberator for all life. In fact, that's the title of an entire movement working to bridge social justice and the environment.

Founded in South America as a way to fight for social change and embrace the plight of the poor, liberation theology is at the core of an ecumenical treatise called, "Liberating Life: A Report to the World Council of Churches." The basis of this theology is to free the abused, as well as the oppressor or privileged who performs the abuse. The main tenet is that "just as it liberates the victimized, humans and other living beings, a theology for the liberation of life can liberate people of privilege and power from their complacency and isolation. A theology that so serves the liberation of life is a theology of justice, peace, and respect for the integrity of creation." At the base of this kind of religious thinking is the belief that Christ died for all life, not just humanity. Whether you subscribe to the idea of Christ or not doesn't matter nearly as much as the radical idea expressed through a theology that could liberate hundreds of millions of people from their institutionalized thinking, dominated by power structures that don't really value equality. The very idea that all life is equal, even in redemption, is powerful if not earth-shattering.

The report goes on to bridge even more gaps, including science and religion:

> The biological theory of evolution with its ingredient of chance and struggle for existence requires a deeper understanding of divine power. God is not a magician but one who lovingly invites the created world to participate in the unfolding of the cosmic story. Evolutionary thinking compels us to acknowledge more explicitly than ever before the continuity of the whole network of life with the universe as such. The evolutionary cosmic epic contributes to a deeper understanding of the universe as our origin and our home.... Our existence is deeply embedded in the existence of the universe itself.

I've long believed Western religion and evolution can get along, and that in fact the two concepts are not and have never been diametrically opposed at their cores. Life is not static, it is dynamic. We can witness this relationship on a micro scale when a larva turns into a chrysalis turns into a butterfly, or when fallen trees decay and become soil, or when trees genetically reprogram themselves to thrive in a still valley or a windy hillside. Life begets life, and life changes. The idea that nature is static is disproved at every turn, and if it were static, it would cease to be a wonder. It would cease to carry joy, purpose, and a spark that ignites our spiritual exploration and the creation of diverse languages to touch and know the Earth. Liberation theology seeks to listen to the voices of the marginalized—prairie dogs, moths, forests, oceans—as well as the voices of those from ethnic, gender, and class minorities. Together, we can take responsibility for honoring the web of life and ensuring we maintain the healthy interconnectedness of diversity, all while addressing environmental and social justice.

Neither science nor religion alone can save us; somewhere in the middle is where we find our common ground. If we believe science and technology alone can solve climate change and avert the inevitable wars and mass migrations, we're deluding ourselves. And if we believe only prayer or incantation or spiritual connection with living organisms can do the same, we're deluding ourselves. Even in the face of scientific evidence that shows we are part of a natural process, we don't believe it. Even in the face of religious texts that teach us to honor, respect, and care for our world made for all of us, we don't believe it. Or, we don't want to believe because it spells the end of our power over ourselves and one another.

Somehow, no matter the insights into our shared lives showing how equally we are made or similarly we live, we strive to divide and conquer. It's disorder, not order, we thrive on. And when we recognize or see coherence in nature, including in ourselves, we run away screaming that it could not be so. How could it be that we are like plants or apes? How could it be that we are field lilies and birds and stardust and mathematical equations? Why do we refuse the stability of equality across all creeds and religions, and across all species and times? How do we overcome our evolutionary-based animal brains that yell at us to compete and fight for survival by subduing the world and others—or rearranging it for our use, whether that use be for protection, nourishment, or decoration? How do we create and foster an ethical evolution that rewires our brains, reimagines our cultures, and reintegrates our psychological and physical languages to cohere with wildness?

It's dangerous on any level to see ourselves as stewards. It reinforces our power, shame, and guilt, while simultaneously giving some degree of credence to our greed and hunger for dominion. How do we find a better balance as a species that wants to interfere and must interfere? When do we hold back and when do we rush in? When do we love and when do we let go as an act of greater love? I propose we can begin to find balance in our gardens. Those intimate spaces are our private battlegrounds for ethical evolution, and while they may be small, gardeners, psychologists, and urban planners know their far-reaching power.

If we garden mostly for ourselves, we deny the languages of other lives and proclaim ourselves the right species in a wrong world. If we garden solely for other species, we risk alienating ourselves from those other species and seeing ourselves as separate from life. If we garden with native plants that form living communities—if we begin to understand the larger systems at play and the systems that still exist even in radically altered urban environments—we begin to cross-pollinate again. We begin to learn to speak languages we've forgotten. We mend. We bind.

If we don't come to see the nonhuman world as primary, we risk losing ourselves physically, mentally, and spiritually. I can't exist without bluestem or prairie dogs or polar bears or salt creek tiger beetles, and neither can you. It's not because they help the world go round (but they do), or that they directly impact my life every day (but they do). Without the existence of other species who thrive without us, we take one step closer to being mentally unhinged, dangerously ill in mind and body in ways we can't begin to imagine. Or can we?

If students perform better in school and cultivate stronger social relationships, if hospital patients recover faster with views of trees and gardens, can't we understand what's at stake? If mangrove forests and swamplands protect us from a hurricane's swell, shouldn't we want to keep those places intact? If we give flowers to a sick loved one or to a person we admire, we're speaking a language of healing and compassion, even if we've decapitated a plant to do so.

Even so, that language often loses something in human translation. For example, I'm astounded by the conversation that says in order to help pollinators we need to use as many flowering plant species as possible, no matter their ecological niche. We need to use these plants to diversify and extend the bloom time in each season, the argument goes. Yet what did native pollinator species like bees do for forage before we brought in exotic species to extend the bloom time? How did bees survive? Were they just barely hanging on? Or is the entire discussion around "extending the bloom time" a deflection from the more pervasive causes of pollinator decline—industrial agriculture, suburbanization, resource extraction, habitat loss, pesticide use—that might uncomfortably implicate us? If we faced the larger issues caused by these forms of human privilege, would we then have to face a total reworking of our culture and our self-identity? Would that shatter our perception of reality and the safety net of our social systems that, in many ways, slowly erode themselves through environmental upheaval?

Perhaps we avoid conservation and revitalization in our landscapes because these practices are at odds with the convenience of how we heat our homes, buy a new car, and communicate. To be an environmental steward is to be fully aware and awakened to how stewardship as we know it has failed in the face of our culture. It's not enough to profess love for nature. We have to—either individually or as a group of individuals—radically and profoundly act with other animals' interests as the core of our own interests. Instead of working hard to validate our preferences for one fair-trade coffee brand over another or shopping at a local shop over an online retailer, we need to understand why we're trying to validate our preferences and also how that validation requires great mental gymnastics in the face of environmental collapse.

Returning to the assertion that using exotic plants is necessary for extending the bloom time for bees, perhaps we're working overtime to prove the benefit of those plants. Maybe we're trying to prove that our aesthetic choices are not as self-important or self-privileging as some would suggest, and that even by potentially doing harm (the possibility for a species to become invasive in time, or provide only minimal ecosystem services), we're also doing some good (a few adult pollinators are using the plant, we're creating beauty that will inspire people, it's better than no plant at all). In the end, we're vitally concerned with trying to make ourselves feel better, to prevent ourselves from falling into the rabbit hole of complex emotion, critical thinking, or too much reality.

But this practice will always prevent us from being the enlightened stewards we imagine ourselves to be. We won't be better, or feel better, if we don't give up the myth of our supremacy. And if it's too much to ask of ourselves to give up this myth in our gardens, it may be too much to ask of ourselves in curbing climate change and mass extinction.

Right now our garden world is caught up in the larger human cultural battle of Enlightenment rationalism and Romanticism. We feel left behind by technology that speedily morphs us all into one culture, as well as an economic system that privileges the individual over the community and the wealthy few over the masses. How can we think ourselves through environmental issues, how can we weave together a multispecies community that thrives on diversity, while ensuring equality and opportunity for all? Especially when that equality starts in our own private kingdoms— our personal gardens? You can see the lines drawn between the competing ideologies of novel ecosystems and revived native plant landscapes: one is labeled rational and the other emotional.

How we navigate environmentalism, how gardens and their larger iterations in parks and refuges connect us to a wildness that jumpstarts our highest democratic ideals, may be an instructive practice for our other human-made institutions. And this environmentalism can't be driven by fact or emotion alone; there must be an interplay between science and belief. As a garden first enraptures us with an abstract sense of beauty and biophilic awe, with life dancing in and out of its shadows, it must also quickly make evident its role as bridge builder between ourselves and other species—and its destiny as a thriving ecosystem.

A garden must be a place of equality that goes beyond human rational or emotional thinking, beyond our sense of right and wrong, beyond our own democracy as a place to welcome all faiths, creeds, and genders. A garden must be a nexus for practicing a social justice rooted in equality for every human, bee, wasp, fly, frog, bird, beetle, and worm that finds its way there. A garden must aim for that perfect balance where the emotional and spiritual inform and are informed by fact and science. Maybe, in the act of creating such a garden, we will finally understand what liberty for all feels like.

I lived in Nebraska for 12 years before I discovered even a fraction of its incredibly diverse landscape. Writing that sentence is as profound a shock to me as it might be to anyone else—not just that I've lived here for 12 years, but that Nebraska has incredible ecological diversity. When I moved from Ohio to Nebraska to begin another graduate degree, I was beyond certain that I would live in the perceived armpit of flyover country for only four or five years—just long enough to complete my coursework and get out, maybe return to Minnesota. Never in a million years did I think I'd end up making my home in the center of the corn and beef industry.

Three events conspired to both keep me in the state and open my eyes, and my soul, to the Great Plains. The first was that my girlfriend at the time, now my wife, followed me out from Ohio to do her own graduate work. The second was performing research for a memoir that took me to parts of Kansas and Oklahoma. The third was a spur-of-the-moment road trip across Nebraska.

My wife and I usually head to Minnesota over the Fourth of July. In Lincoln, the holiday brings out artillery of the kind that literally sends veterans into their basements (I know, I've talked to them). For two straight nights, Lincoln is awash in violent flares of color and percussion shots that move dishes in the kitchen cabinet. One neighbor stores something like a hundred boxes of explosives in his basement beginning in early spring, then puts on a show that sees the streets clogged with parked cars on both sides for a quarter mile in any direction. But in 2015 my mother was still in the early period of recovering from spinal surgery, so we had to find an alternate exodus.

For years my wife and I traveled each March to see the seven-million-year-old sandhill crane migration in central Nebraska, which is not more than ninety minutes from our door. We park our car among the stubble of last year's cornfields and watch as tens of thousands of massive birds wander the rows pecking at fallen corn kernels, then lift in great gray masses, calling to each other in a voice so ancient that the world doesn't seem recognizable. At sunset the entire population along a twenty-mile stretch of the Platte River rises from the fields to circle and settle on sandbars in the water. It was with this inspiration in mind that my wife suggested a quick three-day tourist cavalcade across the western reaches of the panhandle, carving through the Sandhills, then coming back home along the northern border once Independence Day had passed.

There's a reason the speed limit on I-80 is 75 miles an hour, and why folks go 85; there's seemingly little to see, and driving the stretch from near the panhandle on into Iowa can be mind-numbing. But most interstates are an endurance race. Get a few miles off I-80 in central or western Nebraska and it's easy to feel you've entered a place that time forgot. The Sandhills bubble up north of the highway and west of Grand Island. In early summer they are a rocking sea of short green grasses with numerous pothole ponds and lakes full from spring rains. Here, the freshwater Ogallala Aquifer that spans many states is nearest the Earth's surface, the only place where it is recharging versus being drawn down exponentially for irrigating crops and quenching cattle's thirst.

It didn't take long for Highway 6 through central Nebraska to erase the memory of eastern Nebraska's mostly flat fields of gold. Trains carrying coal from Wyoming line the base of hills near the road, coming east at regular and constant intervals. Honestly, it feels like the western coast of Ireland, looking out across the pond toward America.

Once you get within sixty minutes of the Wyoming border, the Sandhills draw down and large rock formations burst upward. Spires of stone and miles of canyon hint that the Rockies are only hours away by car. But it's not these places that stirred my spirit and altered my perception of Nebraska, and even the entire Plains. While the sand dunes and sharp outcroppings helped me see a new world, it was far northwest Nebraska that broke me open to what home has always been for me, though I seldom experience it.

We were on our way to Toadstool Geologic Park, in the Oglala National Grassland only miles away from South Dakota. If you've seen pictures of a long two-lane, black asphalt road rolling off into the distance, flanked by green grasslands with a slate-blue sky, then you begin to understand where I was—and why halfway to some small town I had never heard of, I pulled the car to the side of the road, got out, leaned against the passenger side, and let myself fall into the place.

There was no sound. Nothing. No cars or planes, no lawn-mowers, no barking dogs, no ambient evidence that humans were here except for the road. I'd never been somewhere so quiet. And yet it was loud. There was this deep richness, like the smell of fresh compost or the air after a heavy spring rainstorm on a warm eve-ning—but it wasn't a smell, it was a sound. The air was thick with life, like the presence of a nearby body, the echo of movement close but imperceptible. I'd even argue the air tasted thicker, not muggy or smoky—no, it was a thickness like pure oxygen.

My wife got out of the car and stood with me. It was only a few minutes, but it might as well have been days or weeks. From somewhere nearby we heard songbirds or grassland birds calling— they could have been a mile away, nothing else intruded on their voices. I didn't want to speak, to force myself on this place or that moment, but I had to. I told my wife I wanted to die here because this was the kind of place where I could fully become myself. I don't remember what she said, or what we said after getting in the car on our way to Agate Fossil Beds National Monument, which was on our way to Toadstool. If you've ever had a moment of pure clarity, of visceral connection that was beyond the tactile and even beyond our language or sense of time, you know what I felt. We hold on to these moments like treasures, embers we stoke the rest of our lives in hopes we have the courage to ignite them into full flames.

But I have a suspicion this Nebraska road trip over a long holiday weekend, touching just the surface of a place I never thought was worth my time, would not have been what it was without my four trips to Oklahoma from 2009 to 2014. Over that time I interviewed family members, visited museums and archives, and walked places wilder than I knew existed growing up my first ten years. I saw the woodlands, green tallgrass, and black soil in northeastern Oklahoma quickly shift to the scraggly oaks, open vistas, and bright red soil of central and western Oklahoma, where cactus and sage grew. I walked part of the Wichita Mountains buried up to their chins with Rocky Mountain sediment over millions of years, spent thirty minutes staring out of our parked car as a lone bison grazed twenty feet away. I spoke with park rangers at the Black Kettle National Grassland near the site where, in 1894, George Armstrong Custer slaughtered the winter village of the Cheyenne peace chief for whom this place is named. And I watched my wife cry over the words of those who survived the attack and felt our intruding silence walking the battleground as prayer cloths flapped in the trees. It was the same silence I felt walking the Dachau concentration camp outside of Munich, Germany.

I know myself through my family—our history of farming the prairie, our indirect role in the radical change of an entire ecosystem that occurred in no more than a decade. I know the cultures that have been eradicated or pushed to the brink, and not just human cultures but entire societies of animals and plants and soil fungi. I know, too, that many of these cultures are waiting, holding on to the fragments we've found no use for—this is why a large part of the Wichita Mountains is an army firing range, and why the Sandhills are unfarmable, and why the Tallgrass Prairie National Preserve exists in the rocky Flint Hills of Kansas. Wildness is among us—and it's not just the robins and blue jays and swallowtails and raccoons. The wildness that can't adapt to our human world is just beyond the wildness that can, and those are the voices I've heard on an empty Nebraska highway and in

a bustling fragment of a prairie dog town in Oklahoma. They're
the voices I hear in acres of tallgrass just outside the city, and, on
occasion, in my own backyard.

Can gardens literally save the world? No. Even if they are linked
together to create some new hybrid habitat—even if that habitat
is mostly native plants—gardens won't make more than a dent in
the thriving ecology of other cultures. But gardens are far from
powerless; in fact, I believe they are a lynchpin to greater steps—
from alternative energy to permaculture—that *will* save the world.
Gardens are exponentially powerful. We are removed from wildness. We are removed from knowing the voices or lives of other
species. We've so quickly and efficiently changed the world to our
uses and our convenience that a different kind of silence permeates
our bodies, one that is as subtly painful as a leg or arm that's fallen
asleep.

Gardens can save the world by saving us. They can bring us
back into contact with diversity. They can do what landscape architects like Olmsted envisioned: bring different cultures together
in an open, democratic space to share their lives and learn from
one another so that they might grow stronger together. Gardens
in our back and front yards, gardens along urban streets, gardens
in suburban parks, gardens surrounding schools and churches
and corporate headquarters. Gardens buzzing and humming and
rustling, forming connected highways of mammals and birds and
pollinators and microbes. Gardens that heal our broken bonds to
nature and to one another. Gardens as activism as surely as any art
form, and as surely as any mercy we might bestow on one another
in times of sorrow or anger. Gardens that stir our senses and give
us actionable faith and hope.

But we should always be wary of hope as a goal of its own, as
it can be as dangerous as privileging beauty in the gardens this
century needs. Both hope and beauty whittle down complex emotions and perceptions to black and white, while simultaneously

smoothing over the roughness of our consciousness and the consciousness of all life. Hope says that, in the end, everything will
be okay and creates a complacency that lacks the urgency to fuel
immediate action. Hope puts off grief and anger and even some
level of interceding compassion. Beauty says life is a vista that primarily soothes and inspires, that how we aesthetically interpret
something is as relevant and important as the inalienable rights at
the core of the lives or places we are judging, if not more so. Beauty
gives worth to not just an experience but the surface composition
of entire species and ecosystems. Like hope, beauty paints a façade
over life so that we feel better about ourselves without having to
do the hard, honest work of critical thinking—and then acting—
to create a revolutionary biophilia within the rough edges of our
existence.

Gardens may give us hope, gardens may give us beauty, but
if this is what we primarily seek or talk about with each other in
these spaces—if hope and beauty are confined to the surface textures, colors, and forms—gardens will never be enough. Gardens
can and should be far, far more. Beauty and hope are in the soil.
They're larvae eating the leaves. They're wasps laying eggs in those
larvae. They're birds feeding insects to their young. They're ants
farming aphids. They're plants giving off VOCs as they communicate with the ecosystem around them. They're coevolved nature
tooth and claw, welcomed into our lives and altering our lives fundamentally, expanding our perspectives, moving our empathy on
to the rest of life, so that in the end loving another life form helps
us love ourselves ten times more. Hope and beauty are the fight
for equality, and they are painful and uncomfortable in their most
revolutionary forms.

I don't want to always feel better in my garden. I don't want to
be healed. I need my pain. I need my anger. These emotions are
not enemies but indicators of empathy and compassion. They let
me know the depth of my feeling and the power of all life strug-
gling for justice and equality. If I deny the full feeling of my being,
I deny the full power of my ability to comprehend and live in a

thriving world. Science tells me we are made of the same stuff, that
we all speak a similar language. Religion tells me the divine, the
numinous, is breathed into every life and landscape. My nature is a
nature of defiance for the bonds we break between us in the name
of power or personal liberty. My freedom is based in the freedom
of other species and other places, even if I never see them. This is
why native plant gardens matter more than we may want to know.

The hellstrip lawn in front of our house is never watered, and as
such, grows so sluggishly that I seldom mow it. The grass becomes
thinner and weeds blow in—crab grass and pricklers and black
medic. Since I mow infrequently, the weeds flower and go to seed.
Come midsummer I'll quickly yank the mower from the corner
of the garage after getting home from running errands and sweep
over the lawn to appease the neighbors. Sometimes I'll even grab
a digger to get at the weeds.

What I should do is rip out the entire bed and replace it with
drought-tolerant native grasses or sedge, even as I realize the small
lawn is an element that ties my landscape into the rest of the suburban landscape. But miracles happen on their own—somehow,
the nature that used to be here dips its toe into the wasteland and
puts down a taproot. Because of the absent mower, a milkweed
sprouted near the property line. The neighbor on that side waters
every single morning, so I'm sure the overspray and runoff helped
the milkweed establish. For weeks as it grew, as four leaves became
eight, I debated moving it to the back gardens. I knew that if I cut
its young taproot it would suffer and perhaps die. Every day that
I waited, the root probably grew by an inch, and I knew if it got
much bigger I'd be getting another letter in the mail.

I'm not often out in the tamed wildness of my front gardens.
I don't like being seen or, perhaps more accurately, I fear being
judged from behind windows reflecting manicured lawns. It's
ironic that I can feel so adamant and confident behind the house
but so unsure out here. It's ironic, too, that those back gardens

are the ones folks gasp over when shown photographs. One day I muster up some courage and grab the soil knife. I quickly stab a circle around the milkweed as far down as I can, about six inches; I feel like I'm stealing someone's mail. I place the plant in the back meadow where it soon withers away in a freakishly hot autumn. Maybe it will come back next summer, maybe it won't. Maybe it will be covered in monarch eggs and milkweed beetles. Maybe its fragrance will reach out beyond this small, insignificant place and make someone stop in their tracks. Maybe they will let another milkweed grow wherever it comes up and help revive the natural world.

I dream of suburban developments in Nebraska where the primary landscape model is drifts of prairie or prairie-style gardens, with lawn as needed for play spaces or drivers' sight lines. I dream of roadsides filled with little bluestem, false indigo, rattlesnake master, coneflowers, and asters swaying in the wind. I dream of strip malls and industrial warehouses surrounded by ribbons of prairie and birds calling from within, mowed paths for workers to wander on break, benches to eat lunch on while butterflies skim over their heads. I dream of downtowns where planting beds flank the sidewalks, treating runoff and helping to cool the environment while providing pollen for native bees. I dream of schools where part of the curriculum uses gardens and revived natural areas as living classrooms for art, science, history, and writing. I dream of a world we actively propagate and welcome into every moment of the day, a world we fight for because we've fallen in love and are willing to stand up for the health and freedom of all creation. And we can dream further and harder than this. We can touch and taste and hear the world around us and know the deepest sorrows as the deepest joys if we are ready to imagine justice and democracy as our hands in the soil.

And yet it can often feel like much of the landscape design world, though not all of it, is far too divorced from the actual ecological processes and communities that still exist in our country, even in urban centers and other novel ecosystems. We can deny those ecological communities all we want, but it won't make us feel any better about our role in climate change or extinction, or lead to effective outcomes. We're getting there as more projects become joint collaborations between architects, engineers, biologists, ecologists, and horticulturists. But if these new gardens do not spur a significant psychological, if not spiritual, ethic grounded in both reverence and science—an ethic that truly links human and animal culture well beyond even biophilic aesthetics—our species will not endure. How we experience and intervene in our daily environment is how we will experience and intervene in our larger world.

I'm going to keep speaking for the voiceless—those species and organisms who no longer have or never had a voice in our consciousness—no matter the cost. From grouse to ferrets, beetles to wasps, I draw the line knowing what that means, what I will lose in this culture. If you believe in climate change, if you believe in extinction, if you believe we have a direct and powerful hand in eroding life, you know you must speak up too—as you know your action must follow that powerful voice. Fight for the last stand of blowout penstemon. Fight for the last prairie dog. Fight for the last woodland. Fight for the last sentence that makes us equal to the beauty and purpose of every organism, as well as the wild knowledge older than our own. You'll have to develop a thick skin, but the stakes could not be higher.

Study and learn, be open to perspectives and research that challenge and make you feel uncomfortable. Celebrate conflicting information and follow the scientific and emotional facts down to the core. Test your assumptions. Test the assumptions of others. Know that every plant and every place matters—a powerful, compassionate realization. Be willing to love with a broken heart, to foster that breaking and touch the world that so many hold at a distance to protect their identity. Be totally vulnerable in your mind, your soul, and your garden. Sit outside on a summer evening and listen—don't speak or move. Ride the sunset down past twilight into the dark starlight. Let your bones chill as crickets and lightning bugs rise from the shadows in their hunger. Every moment is an opportunity to wake from ourselves, but we must be as deliberate as crickets and lightning bugs in doing so. And when we are this deliberate, nothing can stop us from changing the world—not even our own fears.

We all have the equal right to exist. We all depend upon one another. We are all an imperfect perfection—every stem, every bloom, every burrow, every cloud, every call, every kiss, every touch. Rise up and love all that we negate through our closed-off culture.

It is time for a garden revolution. It is time for daily wildness to be our calling. It is time for defiant compassion.

Notes

Chapter 1: A New Garden Ethic

1. Deep ecology is well worth studying as a way to open our perspective in unfamiliar yet connective ways. *Deep Ecology: Living as if Nature Mattered* is a good starting point, as is *The Rights of Nature*. While deep ecology may not at first appear practical, it is crucial toward rewiring our culture and rethinking how we engage with, manage, and revive wildness. In essence, deep ecology is a simultaneous study of the spiritual and the scientific, bridging the gap between the left and right brain.

2. A helpful starting point to explore how our default landscaping mode, traditional lawns, are dangerous for the environment can be found in *American Green* by Ted Steinberg. His book explores the history of lawns, their repercussions, and how to better use these green spaces.

3. The term for this new epoch, replacing the Holocene that began 11,700 years ago, was popularized by atmospheric chemist and Nobel laureate Paul Crutzen in 2000. The Anthropocene marks a time when humanity's influence is global and apparent over every last square inch. Scientists suggest it should begin with the dawn of nuclear weapon tests and the spread of radioactive material across the world, but it could also be marked by pollution from industrial electricity generation and factories, or even plastic trash.

Chapter 2: More Than Native Plants

1. Defining native plants is often a highly charged exercise. Sometimes the definition can feel subjective or based on emotion, especially if it confronts our preconceptions, belief system, or sense of self. And yet science shows us the role of indigenous plants within an ecosystem and their relationships with other flora and fauna over time, and science is certainly not subjective. A definition of native plants is arbitrary, however, in the same way that the definition of species or mountain or river is arbitrary. We decide how to define the terms we use, but we don't decide how the natural world works. In urban

165

areas, we are just beginning to understand the role native and exotic plants play for countless ecosystem services, and the degree of benefit for those services, including supporting wildlife.

2. Global honey bee populations are actually stable, even though some regions have experienced recent declines. For an in-depth look at the status of bees and pollinators, see "The Assessment Report on Polli- nators, Pollinations, and Food Production" from the IPBES (Inter- governmental Science-Policy Platform on Biodiversity and Ecosys- tem Services), nora.nerc.ac.uk/514356/1/N514356CR.pdf

    As for competition, James Cane and Vincent Tepedino in "Gaug- ing the Effect of Bee Pollen Collection on Native Bee Communi- ties" discover that one hive of honey bees in three months collects as much forage as 100,000 solitary native bees over the same time. Backyard hives may do more harm than good for our best pollina- tors. It's estimated that one acre of diverse forage is needed to sustain one honey bee hive.

    Another study led by Sandra A.M. Lindstrom suggests honey bee hives diminish numbers of various flower-visiting insects, and may have implications for crop pollination and pollinator health. The study is titled "Experimental Evidence That Honeybees Depress Wild Insect Densities in a Flowering Crop."

    In regards to a bee's ability to adapt when their preferred flowers are absent or minimal, some bees show behavioral plasticity and will more easily seek out other blooms. But as species diversify their flower portfolio, they increase the risk of transmitting diseases to one another. Flowers are reservoirs for parasites and increase trans- mission between bee species. In other words, flower abundance is key to bee health, for this reason and many others, including self- medication and protein content. For more, see the piece "The Com- plex Causes of Worldwide Bee Declines," and note the sources cited.

3. To learn more about prairie dogs, their history, culture, and ecologi- cal role within the Great Plains environment, Paul Johnsgard's book *Prairie Dog Empire* is an indispensable resource.

Chapter 3: Why We Believe What We Believe

1. In his *Guardian* piece "Generation Anthropocene," author Robert Macfarlane explores how contemporary art—including film and tele- vision—is exploring and confronting the reality of our new epoch. Ultimately, the way our arts address climate change and extinction

helps us expand philosophically by breaking down binaries like nature and culture.

2. A phrase that's been circulating among social justice advocates the last few years has been, "When you're accustomed to privilege, equality feels like oppression." While it's not certain who coined this phrase, the idea is apt beyond usage for issues of human privilege (white, straight, rich, et cetera). In the context of gardening for wildlife—privileging the needs of animal species in a design—it might feel uncomfortable, even alienating, because humans so often privilege themselves over other species and landscapes.

Chapter 4: Urban Wildness and Social Justice

1. With at least a hundred cultivars on the market, if not closer to two hundred, butterfly bush is here to stay in the horticulture trade (both southwest natives and global exotics). And you'll find no limit to the number of opinions and research on the efficacy of these plants outside of their native range. A study by Julie Ream looked at invasiveness of the most common *Buddleja davidii* in Oregon, and how growers there prune plants before seeds become viable in winter, so invasion is likely coming from private and public landscape plantings.

    Another study by Joseph Culin explored how certain cultivars of *B. davidii* are more attractive to pollinators based on flower color and nectar quality. However, the study did not make comparisons to native plants. Other studies explore seed weight and germination rates for certain cultivars, showing that some establish more easily than others, particularly in disturbed areas like roadsides, river edges, train tracks, fields, et cetera. Climate change will also play a role, with the northeastern United States and southeastern Canada most likely to see butterfly bush spread in the wild. I suggest performing a Google Scholar search to fully explore the available research on the pros and cons of using butterfly bush in North America.

2. A good introductory exploration of the history of landscape architecture is Elizabeth Barlow's *Landscape Design: A Cultural and Architectural History*.

Chapter 5: Speaking the Language Again

1. There are several books on plant communities, even how they evoke an echo of human communication and survival. One such book is

What a Plant Knows by Daniel Chamovitz. Another, which explores other science-based reasons for why plants act the way they do, is Linda Chalker-Scott's *How Plants Work*.

2. The intersections of human and landscape language, or human and landscape culture, are explored in two books by Native American authors that have been formative to my thinking: *The Man Made of Words* by N. Scott Momaday and *Dwellings* by Linda Hogan. Both authors have their feet grounded in two worlds—the Western and the Native, the self and the other.

Suggested Reading

Environmental Philosophy, Psychology, and Science

The Spell of the Sensuous: Perception and Language in a More-Than-Human World. David Abram (Vintage, 1997)

Silent Spring. Rachel Carson (Houghton Mifflin, 2002)

What a Plant Knows: A Field Guide to the Senses. Daniel Chamovitz (Scientific American, 2013)

Uncommon Ground: Rethinking the Human Place. Ed. William Cronon (W. W. Norton & Company, 1996)

Deep Ecology: Living as if Nature Mattered. Bill Devall and George Sessions (Gibbs Smith, 1985)

The Ecocriticism Reader: Landmarks in Literary Ecology. Eds. Cheryll Glotfelty and Harold Fromm (The University of Georgia Press, 1996)

This Sacred Earth: Religion, Nature, Environment. Ed. Roger Gottlieb (Routledge, 2003)

Greater Perfections: The Practice of Garden Theory. John Dixon Hunt (University of Pennsylvania Press, 2000)

Is Shame Necessary? New Uses for an Old Tool. Jennifer Jacquet (Pantheon, 2015)

The Derrick Jensen Reader: Writings on Environmental Revolution. Ed. Lierre Keith (Seven Stories Press, 2012)

This Changes Everything: Capitalism vs the Climate. Naomi Klein (Simon & Schuster, 2015)

The Sixth Extinction: An Unnatural History. Elizabeth Kolbert (Picador, 2015)

A Sand County Almanac. Aldo Leopold (Ballantine Books, 1986)

Last Child in the Woods: Saving Our Children from Nature-Deficit Disorder. Richard Louv (Algonquin Books, 2008)

Coming Back to Life: Practices to Reconnect Our Lives, Our World. Joanna Macy and Molly Young Brown (New Society Publishers, 1998)

The Rambunctious Garden: Saving Nature in a Post-Wild World. Emma Marris (Bloomsbury, 2011)

The End of Nature. Bill McKibben (Anchor Books, 1989)

Moral Ground: Ethical Action for a Planet in Peril. Eds. Kathleen Dean
   Moore and Michael P. Nelson (Trinity University Press, 2010)
The Rights of Nature: A History of Environmental Ethics. Roderick Nash
   (University of Wisconsin Press, 1989)
The Green Boat: Reviving Ourselves in Our Capsized Culture. Mary
   Pipher (Riverhead Books, 2013).
Plant Conservation: Why It Matters and How It Works. Timothy Walker
   (Timber Press, 2013)
Half-Earth: Our Planet's Fight for Life. E.O. Wilson (Liveright, 2016)
The Art of the Commonplace: The Agrarian Essays of Wendell Berry.
   ed. Norman Wirzba (Counterpoint, 2003)

Landscape Design, Native Plants, and Wildlife
Principles of Ecological Landscape Design. Travis Beck (Island Press, 2013)
*The New American Landscape: Leading Voices on the Future of Sustainable
   Gardening.* Ed. Thomas Christopher (Timber Press, 2011)
*The Living Landscape: Designing for Beauty and Biodiversity in the Home
   Garden.* Rick Darke and Doug Tallamy (Timber Press, 2014).
The Know Maintenance Perennial Garden. Roy Diblik (Timber Press,
   2014)
Hellstrip Gardening: Create a Paradise Between the Sidewalk and the Curb.
   Evelyn Hadden (Timber Press, 2014)
Bees: An Identification and Native Plant Forage Guide. Heather Holm
   (Pollination Press, 2017)
*Pollinators of Native Plants: Attract, Observe and Identify Pollinators and
   Beneficial Insects with Native Plants.* Heather Holm (Pollination Press,
   2014)
The Shape of Green: Aesthetics, Ecology, and Design. Lance Hosey (Island
   Press, 2012)
Planting: A New Perspective. Piet Oudolf and Noel Kingsbury (Timber
   Press, 2013)
*Lawn Gone! Low-Maintenance, Sustainable, Attractive Alternatives for
   Your Yard.* Pam Penick (Ten Speed Press, 2013)
*Planting in a Post-Wild World: Designing Plant Communities for Resilient
   Landscapes.* Thomas Rainer and Claudia West (Timber Press, 2015)
*Energy-Wise Landscape Design: A New Approach for Your Home and
   Garden.* Sue Reed (New Society Publishers, 2010)
Wild by Design: Strategies for Creating Life-Enhancing Landscapes. Margie
   Ruddick (Island Press, 2016)

Bringing Nature Home: How You Can Sustain Wildlife with Native Plants.
Douglas Tallamy (Timber Press, 2009)
Attracting Native Pollinators: Protecting North America's Bees and Butter-flies. The Xerces Society (Storey Publishing, 2011)
Gardening for Butterflies: How You Can Attract and Protect Beautiful, Beneficial Insects. The Xerces Society (Timber Press, 2016)
Attracting Beneficial Bugs to Your Garden: A Natural Approach to Pest Control. Jessica Walliser (Timber Press, 2013)
Garden Revolution: How Our Landscapes Can Be a Source of Environmental Change. Larry Weaner and Thomas Christopher (Timber Press, 2016)

Prairie and the Great Plains

Jewels of the Plains: Wildflowers of the Great Plains, Grasslands, and Hills. Claude Barr, ed. James Locklear (University of Minnesota Press, 2015)
Field Guide to the Wildflowers of Nebraska and the Great Plains. Jon Farrar (University of Iowa Press, 2011)
Great Plains: America's Lingering Wild. Michael Forsberg (University of Chicago Press, 2009)
The Ecology and Management of Prairies in the Central United States. Chris Helzer (University of Iowa Press, 2009)
Grassland: The History, Biology, Politics, and Promise of the American Prairie. Richard Manning (Penguin, 1997)
Prairie: A Natural History. Candace Savage (Greystone Books, 2011)
Big Bluestem: A Journey into the Tallgrass. Annick Smith (Council Oak Books, 1996)

Acknowledgments

As an introvert, social media has connected me to diverse people and meaningful conversations without having to leave the joy of my home and garden. The ability to write out my ideas, to absorb others' thoughts on the page in careful ways, has been my ticket to critical thinking in this manuscript. On many days, I'd begin writing a response to someone and instead copy and paste that response into this book. Other days, our collective voices would seed entire pages that poured out in a matter of minutes. I was pushed and questioned, made as uncomfortable as I was making others, and grew in the often heated back and forth.

I want to thank a few of the people I most vividly recall from online and in-person conversations, knowing that I'm missing so very many to whom I'll owe drinks or solar panels: Kathryn Aalto, Eric Berg, Allen Bush, Susan Cohan, Thomas Christopher, Steve Edwards, Justin Evertson, Solomon Gamboa, James Golden, Graham Gardner, Susan Harris, Bob Henricksen, Heather Holm, Saxon Holt, Frank Hyman, Panayoti Kalaidis, Craig Limpach, Beatriz Moisset, Carrie Preston, Thomas Rainer, Fran Sorin, Tony Spencer, Mark Turner, Claudio Vazquez, and Jan Whitney.

I owe a debt to my team members at the now-defunct blog Native Plants and Wildlife Gardens, which provided years of early encouragement and a wealth of knowledge from around the country.

I especially want to thank Vincent Vizachero, who looked at a portion of the manuscript, and Evelyn Hadden, whose editorial eye was immeasurably valuable throughout. There are also many who left important comments on my blog over the years, the slightly more formal place where I developed and tested ideas in early drafts of this manuscript.

To those who've invited me to speak at conferences and symposiums, and those who've listened then talked with me afterward, you and your stories are an inspiration. I am thankful to meet you. To my editor Ingrid Witvoet at New Society Publishers, who jumped on an online comment I made and asked for a phone call.

To my parents, Debra and Terry, who encouraged every path I've taken and made sure their kids had the world if they worked for it. I couldn't have done any better.

To my wife Jaclyn, who has helped me work through the deeply emotional effects of this book, who is a soulful sounding board, and who is a saint for living with a writer. Let's go find our prairie home.

To the woods and the lakes and the grasslands that have punched me in the gut.

And to those fighting for wildness and freedom for all species through gardens of all kinds.

Index

About the Author

BENJAMIN VOGT owns Monarch Gardens, a prairie garden design firm in Nebraska. His writing and photography have appeared in *Houzz, Nebraska Life, Northern Gardener, Orion, The Sun, Creative Nonfiction,* and books such as *Gardening for Butterflies* (Xerces Society) and *The Tallgrass Prairie Reader.* Benjamin has a PhD from the University of Nebraska-Lincoln, an MFA from the Ohio State University, and speaks widely on native plants, wildlife, and sustainable garden design. He and his wife currently live in Lincoln and dream of reviving 40–80 acres of prairie, complete with artist residency, a sizable native plant display garden, and an off-grid home.

ABOUT NEW SOCIETY PUBLISHERS

New Society Publishers is an activist, solutions-oriented publisher focused on publishing books for a world of change. Our books offer tips, tools, and insights from leading experts in sustainable building, homesteading, climate change, environment, conscientious commerce, renewable energy, and more—positive solutions for troubled times.

We're proud to hold to the highest environmental and social standards of any publisher in North America. This is why some of our books might cost a little more. We think it's worth it!

DON'T EAT THIS BOOK *(but you could)*

- We print all our books in North America, never overseas

- All our books are printed on 100% **post-consumer recycled paper**, processed chlorine-free, with low-VOC vegetable-based inks (since 2002)

- Our corporate structure is an innovative employee shareholder agreement, so we're one-third employee-owned (since 2015)

- We're carbon-neutral (since 2006)

- We're certified as a B Corporation (since 2016)

At New Society Publishers, we care deeply about *what* we publish—but also about *how* we do business.

New Society Publishers
ENVIRONMENTAL BENEFITS STATEMENT

For every 5,000 books printed, New Society saves the following resources:[1]

20	Trees
1,772	Pounds of Solid Waste
1,949	Gallons of Water
2,543	Kilowatt Hours of Electricity
3,221	Pounds of Greenhouse Gases
14	Pounds of HAPs, VOCs, and AOX Combined
5	Cubic Yards of Landfill Space

[1]Environmental benefits are calculated based on research done by the Environmental Defense Fund and other members of the Paper Task Force who study the environmental impacts of the paper industry.

Certified B Corporation

MIX
Paper from responsible sources
FSC
www.fsc.org
FSC® C016245

new society
PUBLISHERS
www.newsociety.com